LIBERATING LEADERSHIP

Practical Styles for Pastoral Ministry

Bernard F. Swain
The Paulist Project

In Collaboration with
Patricia Dunn
James Gorman
William Kondrath

1817

Harper & Row, Publishers, San Francisco

Cambridge, Hagerstown, New York, Philadelphia, Washington
London, Mexico City, São Paulo, Singapore, Sydney

FIRST EDITION

Library of Congress Cataloging-in-Publication Data

Swain, Bernard F.
  Liberating leadership.

  1. Christian leadership. 2. Pastoral theology.
I. Title.
BV652.1.S93   1986   253   86-14879
ISBN 0-86683-483-4

---

86 87 88 89 90 MPC 10 9 8 7 6 5 4 3 2 1

TO ANNE

Who makes me deserve whatever
sense I make.

Contents

Part III
Choosing a Leadership Style

Acknowledgments

This study of the changing "corporate culture" of pastoral leadership is the work of one writer but many minds, and should itself be regarded as a product of collaboration.

The initial insight that pastoral leaders were struggling to combine different styles of leadership came from Pat Dunn, my colleague at the Paulist Project, who looked beyond the symptoms of interpersonal conflict among our clients to discover the emergence of deeper, more systemic dynamics. We first identified this emergence by distinguishing parallel and mutual styles, later rounding out the analysis by reference to sovereign and semimutual styles.

Jim Gorman, also of the Paulist Project, nudged us to adopt the label *sovereign style* in place of an earlier, less neutral name. He and colleague Bill Kondrath then helped us to flesh out the analysis of each style by suggesting relevant factors to be examined and by offering specific details for some of that examination. The result of all this teamwork was the overview grid (see pages 126-127) that was the basis for my writing.

Other Paulist Project staff helped in other capacities. Charlie Martin, C.S.P., and Marie Killilea, C.S.J., helped to organize, type, and word-process the first two drafts of the manuscripts. Bob Lindsay, S.J., joined them in the tedious work of reviewing, proofreading, and editing theses drafts, which were greatly improved by their revisions. Bob and Marie also took responsibility for encouragement and moral support whenever the writer's energies, enthusiasm, or patience failed. Chris

Keenan, OFM, also helped with some editing of the chapter on supervision, and Mark Reamer helped in typing some final sections.

Throughout the thirty-month period of writing and rewriting, ongoing discussion among ourselves and with clients was an indispensable influence in refining the final product. This discussion was especially important in learning how to express the neutrality of our analysis, which does not favor any style, and also in developing the notion of *recipe* (and the related application of *ideal type*) spelled out in Chapter 6. I could not have produced this text without such teammates and clients, for that discussion was their grace to me.

Introduction

This book attempts to draw some simple, general lessons from the working experience of the Paulist Project. This Project has offered a wide range of consultation, training, and renewal services to more than one hundred fifty clients over the past ten years. Our clients have included parish staffs, parish councils, parish renewal committees, religious education programs, schools, religious communities, regional clusters of churches, seminaries, campus chaplaincies, and diocesan offices.

Our work with these clients has had one common theme: to promote the ongoing renewal of the Church, especially in the areas of ministry and leadership. Our clients have invited us to share their struggle to discover, explore, and develop more effective ways to be the Church, to serve the Church, and to lead the Church. These struggles have produced many success stories and a few failures—but every one of these struggles has helped us learn more about how the Church can grow to be at once "ever changing" and yet "always the same."

A chief lesson we have drawn from our common struggle has been the realization that the key to renewing any area of Church life is to develop, not the right structure or the right label or the right people, but the right *style*. This book applies that lesson to the area of Church leadership. Part I explains why style is important. Part II explores the basic styles of ministerial leadership. Part III suggests practical steps toward choosing and building your own style of ministerial leadership.

We have chosen the title *Liberating Leadership* to make two points at once: First, the model we present charts a course by which pastoral leaders can liberate *themselves* from the restrictions, often self-imposed, which prevail in many local pastoral settings; second, the model suggests how leaders can liberate *others* for leadership and ministry.

In our work we repeatedly observe leaders struggling to overcome obstacles of their own making. Some leaders fall into the rut of depending too much on a single style of leadership. Most pastoral settings require leaders to practice different styles under different circumstances, but many leaders are comfortable and confident with only one style and therefore tend to get stuck in it. This model will offer options for getting out of that rut.

Other leaders, unsure of themselves or their setting, or simply unaware of other options, tend to lock themselves into the bind of operating in a style that is not appropriate for the setting they are in. This model offers the opportunity to reassess one's pastoral situation and develop a better match between setting and style.

Finally, many pastoral leaders back themselves into a corner of a random, haphazard pattern of varying their leadership styles. Unsure where to go next at any given point, such leaders alternate styles with no clear rationale. This model can help them to develop a more deliberate and intentional approach to style, resulting in a more consistent and reliable leadership pattern.

This model also enables leaders to empower others for leadership and ministry. By giving leaders a variety of style options, it helps them respond flexibly and effectively to the great variety of people, gifts, and conditions in their setting. By promoting more consistent patterns of behavior, the model helps leaders become more predictable and more reliable in their practice, thus enabling others to know (1) what kind of support they can expect from their leadership and (2) how they can get that support. By enabling leaders to be more deliberate and intentional in choosing their leadership style, this model makes the practice of leadership easier to articulate and communicate and thus helps leaders model leadership to others.

Since our staff first began to develop this model for pastoral leadership, we have tested and refined it against the practical experience of a wide range of pastoral leaders, including the Field Education Supervisors of the Boston Theological Institute (March 1981); the Senior Ministry Candidates of Weston School of Theology (September 1981); the Field Project Sponsors for the Lay Ministry Training Institute, Boston (1981-1986); the Field Education Orientation group, Weston School of Theology (September 1982); the Vicariate for Community Affairs of the Diocese of Providence (September 1982); the School for Deacons of the Episcopal Diocese of Rhode Island (1982-1986); the Parish Outreach Staff for Catholic Charities of the Diocese of Manchester (December 1982); the Advanced Seminar for Field Education Supervisors, Weston School of Theology (February 1983); the Institute for Supervised Ministries, Boston (June 1983); the Annual Community Congress of the Sisters of St. Anne (August 1983); the Annual Conference of the National Association of Lay Ministers (June 1984); the Diocesan Cabinet of the Diocese of Syracuse (October 1984); the Parish *Renew* Teams of the Archdiocese of Denver (June 1985); and a variety of parish staffs, including St. Augustine's Church (Andover, Mass.), St. Gabriel's Church (Brighton, Mass.), Blessed Sacrament Parish (Jamaica Plain, Mass.), St. Joseph Parish (Malden, Mass.), and St. Pius V (Lynn, Mass.).

In testing this model with such a variety of clients, we have found that they quickly acquire a new ability to identify, name, and communicate issues of leadership style. They can share the experience of various styles in their personal career histories. They can articulate their personal preferences about leadership style. They can begin to construct a clear image of the recipe for leadership style that might best meet their current needs. They can engage their peers in building a new consensus about this recipe and about the process they should follow to implement it.

Our aim in writing this book is to convey those same benefits to a wider readership. However, this book is designed not only for parish clergy, parish staffs, and parish councils. Our clients have taught us that leadership styles are equally relevant to religious communities, seminarians, field education supervisors, anyone involved in ministry formation (for clergy, religious, deacons, lay professionals, volunteers, etc.), and professionals involved in retreat work, campus ministry, clinical settings, and diocesan agencies and offices. Nor is the book addressed only to those in Roman Catholic ministry; the issues of leadership style confront ministers in a wide range of denominations. These leaders inhabit different settings and face different issues and concerns; their own behavioral patterns, however, are subject to surprisingly similar influences, and the choices they face in liberating themselves and others are remarkably common. Such choices must be made by leaders themselves; this book can provide only a vocabulary, some guidance, and a good deal of encouragement.

Part I

Leadership Style as an Issue in Pastoral Renewal

Chapter 1

Vatican II:
Still Waiting After All These Years

Perhaps the chief (and currently the most poignant) irony of the era of Vatican II is that, twenty years after the close of the Council, we are still preparing for it.

It is true, of course, that the work of the Council has made a vast difference in the life of ordinary Catholics everywhere. The reform of liturgy has been so sweeping that many lapsed Catholics, returning to weddings or funerals or baptisms after fifteen or twenty years' absence, literally feel they are in a different Church. The work of religious education has been almost completely transformed. Religious life has greatly changed, both within religious communities and in their relations with the Church and world at large. Laity have emerged into new roles of leadership, both as volunteers and as professional ministers. The Church as a whole now presents a remarkably modern face compared to the face of the Church a short generation ago. All this seems quite obvious, even to the casual observer.

What is less obvious, even to the careful observer, is that much of the work of renewal remains unfinished because many Catholics in many places still do not really understand or want renewal in their lives or in their Church.

So the Church still struggles to establish renewal as a priority. Music ministers still appeal to congregations to get them to sing at liturgies. Parents still complain that they no longer know what to teach their kids. *Community* has been the watchword of parish life for nearly a generation, yet for many parishes community is still limited to handshakes and bingo. Parishioners still wonder what parish councils are for—and when they ask an elected council member, they discover that she or he is wondering the same thing. Many Catholics know that the Church now favors ecumenism, but most still don't know what that really means, and many still have little more to do with other traditions than Catholics did a generation ago. Catholics still perceive their faith too often as a series of moral precepts, and many still center that morality on sex. Confessors still struggle to introduce penitents to the new Rite of Reconciliation. Parishioners can be found everywhere who still approach the sacraments as formalities of social custom, with little or no bearing on their real lives.

In short, despite the sweeping innovations since 1962, despite a process for implementing those innovations that has transformed the face of the Church, and despite exceptional success stories of renewal, parish life in many parts of North America is still waiting for renewal to take root.

This is not, I believe, because the Council has failed —though some insist it has. After all, Vatican II was the first ecumenical council to attempt to reexamine the Church's own identity *as* Church. With twenty centuries of Church history behind us, we should not expect such a project to succeed—or fail!—within a single generation.

Nor is the delay in renewal taking root due simply to people resisting the changes wrought by the Council— though many have resisted them. In fact, much of the struggling we have witnessed is happening, not in conservative settings that resist change, but in progressive

settings where people have embraced change but then
have been dissatisfied with the results.

Nor is the delay due simply to changes being rejected
or ineffective once accepted—though some are both.
Indeed, many who are convinced of the value and wis-
dom of those changes nonetheless find renewal just as
much a struggle as do those troubled by the changes.

No, the basic reason why we continue to prepare
people, even now, for changes mandated a generation
ago is at once simpler and more basic than the reasons
just noted. Put simply, most people were never prepared for those changes in the first place!

Once stated, this fact of Catholic life since the Council is so obvious that we might wonder why we didn't
notice it all along. It seems incredible that anyone could
really have expected an institution as ancient, complex,
and massive as the Roman Catholic Church to undergo
rapid and widespread renewal without some kind of
thorough and systematic process designed to prepare
people for the changes to come. Yet the Council fathers
seem to have expected precisely that, for they charted
just such a renewal in the documents of the Council, yet
they planned no process for preparing people prior to
the actual implementation of the Council's reforms.

We can imagine, of course, how the Council's work
might have included thorough preparation, so that the
renewal of the Church would have been accomplished
in three carefully planned stages.

In the first stage, the grand design of the renewal to
be accomplished would be mapped out (much as it actually was in the documents of Vatican II).

In the second stage, people at all levels of Catholic life
would undergo a process (no doubt lengthy and gradual) of preparing for the renewal to come. This preparation process would involve several things: first, the
opportunity to become aware of both the changes that
were to come and the historical and pastoral reasons

behind them; second, the training people needed (given their respective roles in the Church) to exploit those changes for their intended benefits and full potential, lest the effort of innovation be squandered or even distorted; third, the development of the support systems people would need to deal with the stress and strain of change and to sustain a functional unity (rather than a polarizing fragmentation) among people who respond differently to the inevitable tension which change brings; finally, the development of ways for people to adjust and adapt to the new awareness, the new skills, and the new needs for support that renewal would be introducing into their lives.

Overlapping this second stage would be a third, in which the innovations envisaged by the grand design of stage one would be implemented according to a process that allowed sufficient time and flexibility to adapt innovations to local needs and to integrate them with established practices as well as with other innovations already in place. This third stage would also be lengthy and gradual, but, if executed with care by people (on all levels of Church life) who had been thoroughly informed and prepared in advance, the work of integrating new forms of Catholic life could then take place in an orderly way. This would ensure, as much as possible, that once in place these changes would become fully operative in the lives of individuals and congregations alike.

This imaginary plan of renewal is, however, quite different from what really happened. For once the Council had forged its grand design, implementation followed, not after a lengthy period of preparation was already underway, but almost immediately.

Often such implementation was preceded by formal (and often perfunctory) announcements that a change was about to take place; sometimes, usually in Sunday sermons, explanations were offered as to what, or why, change could be expected. But these seldom really prepared people for the changes, for several reasons: First, people seldom felt fully informed about the historical circumstances or pastoral motivations leading to specific changes; second, people were seldom ready either to exploit particular changes or (in the case of more conservative Catholics) even to accept change in general; third, people were not given time to adjust to these changes, to deal with renewal as a process. In fact, implementation usually followed very quickly upon initial announcements—often within weeks.

None of this was anybody's fault; such difficulties were built into our systems of Church life. For one thing, sermons were too short to convey complex histories and decisions, and other adult learning opportunities were too infrequent or reached too few. Also, the recent tradition of a pastorally passive laity created a residual resistance to the more participative style of many Council reforms.

Moreover, the Council's reforms were implemented at a rapid pace. The major changes in eucharistic liturgy were in place by 1970; the major shift in religious education came by the early 1970s; most innovations in the various sacramental rites were completed by the mid-1970s. Given this pace, the inability of announcements and explanations really to prepare people was probably inevitable.

In any case, the result was that much of the work of implementing Vatican II has fallen on pastoral settings that were not ready for it and still are not ready for it. Many Catholics over the last twenty years have found changes already in place without really understanding or being ready for them. Systematic preparation of individuals and communities has often occurred after the fact (in a remedial fashion) if at all. Indeed, much of our work at the Paulist Project involves providing parishes (and other Church agencies) with just such remedial help. We invest a great deal of energy in educating, training, and consulting with clergy and congregations so they can better exploit the promise of the Council's reforms—a promise that too often remains latent rather than operative.

Chapter 2

Reform Without Renewal: Superficial Change and the Unfinished Agenda

In observing that after Vatican II the cart (implementing of the Council's reforms) came before the horse (preparing the people for renewal), I intend no criticism or indictment of the Council, its work, or its consequences. In all probability, this sequence was both historically inevitable and pastorally necessary.

The Council took most people—including most Council fathers—by surprise, and perhaps this element of surprise was key to the Council's success. Maybe the opening of the windows of the Church, so urgently desired by John XXIII, required a sudden gust that could not be channeled. After all, John's calling of the Council stunned the bishops, and the Council proceedings suggest that many bishops had little insight into the long-range consequences implied in their decisions. Would they have been as decisive had they been more farsighted, or would their vision of a Church transformed by the Council have frightened them into more timid initiatives? If local leaders and parishioners had known what was coming, would they have received renewal warmly? Or would they have been "forewarned and forearmed," thus stiffening their opposition to change before it began? My guess is that the sudden and unprepared transformation we underwent during the 1960s and 1970s was the best outcome we could have realistically expected. Certainly it could have been worse. We now tend to take the documents of Vatican II for granted, but the renewal they chart was by no means an automatic result. Once we recall what a remarkable transformation transpired during the Council itself, we realize that a less-than-perfect implementation process is a small price to pay.

We should not, then, regard the need to prepare people for renewal in the wake of the Council's reforms as a problem but simply as the unfinished agenda of the era of Vatican II. Nonetheless we must recognize that finishing that agenda is an urgent pastoral need. For as long as the agenda remains unfinished, we face several risks.

The first, most obvious risk is that people may begin to perceive the existing state of reform as a permanent condition, mistaking an external and sometimes superficial set of reforms for the final, permanent outcome of the Council.

This is sheer delusion. What has been accomplished so far since the Council is, of course, a terrific alteration of the face of the Church. We have witnessed the development of new structures, new regulations, new forms and rites and customs, new law. But the primary intention of the Council fathers who sought renewal was not to alter the *face* of the Church in a purely external way. They aimed, rather, to change and renew the *heart* of the Church: the people themselves. They realized that external changes were merely means to that end, that reforms were merely means to the end called renewal.

Nonetheless many communities have fallen prey to experiments that, while worthy in themselves, trivialized renewal by focusing on superficial change. One obvious example is the relentless flux of textbooks in religious education during the 1970s. How many religious education teachers were led to believe that a new

textbook would cure all the ills of catechism indoctrina-
tion, only to find the new book itself replaced before a
single child could go through the series? Such experiments resulted not in renewed parish life but only in a
new parish program or structure or practice or organization. The risk is that such changes, necessary as they
may be, might delude people into believing that they
have already accomplished parish renewal.

A second, related risk follows. Once people are
deluded into mistaking reforms for renewal, two different, but equally dangerous, responses can emerge.

Some people begin to think and talk of "the failure of
Vatican II." What such people perceive as a final outcome of Vatican II does not match their vision of what
renewal means. Other people, meanwhile, learn to
accept and live with the current reforms. They become
accustomed to the current state of reform as *the* norm
for Catholic living. Though they may feel that the
norm does not really work, they accept its inadequacies
and failures as the best that can be done until some new
reform replaces it.

In both cases, people have moved from the delusion
that the Council's work is done to disillusion with the
Council itself. The first group is disillusioned because it
seems to them that the changes wrought by the Council
have failed to deliver on the renewal it promised. The
second group, even more dangerously, is disillusioned
with the whole idea of renewal, for the changes they
perceive as the Council's work merely provide a new
system for Church life. People in this latter group often
feel that the new system works no better than the old
system did.

The third and final risk of leaving the Council's
agenda unfinished is that, the longer reforms remain in
place without people being prepared to integrate them,
the greater is the risk that the reforms will never be
integrated at all. Treated as ends in themselves, many

of the reforms not only trivialize but even endanger renewal. Once people equate the reforms with renewal itself, their subsequent disillusionment may ensure (either consciously or unconsciously) that they deny the need or value of any renewal. Some will say it is too late, that the Council has already failed. Others will say we have already done the best we can, that we have changed enough. Still others will express how weary they are of the changes, along with how doubtful they are that further change will improve matters. Deluded into believing that renewal merely swaps one system for another, they wonder why we would bother with renewal at all.

On balance, it was good that the Council's reforms were implemented even before people were prepared for renewal. But now the latter task requires urgent attention, since leaving the reforms alone in place risks a process in which people begin with the delusion that renewal is mere external reform, become disillusioned by the results of reform, and end up denying that the work of renewal must go on. The process is self-fulfilling, for if there is a widespread perception that the current state of Conciliar reforms is permanent, it will become permanent.

In short, the process of renewal since the Council has tended to promote reforms without renewal and superficial changes without change in depth. Left unaltered, such a process gives the appearance of renewal without its reality, which, in turn, leads to delusion, disillusion, and even denial. The danger is that the process will end by giving renewal itself a bad name, thus leaving the Council's agenda permanently unfinished.

Given these risks, how are we to avoid the danger which flows from them? Our response is that we should learn from and build upon the many examples of renewal succeeding in local churches. Many parishes and Church communities, of course, experience the process of renewal in a way quite different from the above analysis of the unfinished agenda. Many parishes in many places throughout North America have sought and found ways to prepare people for a way of Christian living that is not only new but rich and meaningful.

Many of these examples come from the great variety of Protestant denominations that have undertaken their own movement of renewal, restructure, and revival. Some of these movements predate Vatican II; others were inspired by it. Still others coincide with Roman Catholic renewal quite independently. In general, it is safe to say that Protestants have longer experience than Catholics in tackling the urgent (and major Conciliar) theme of the Church in the modern world. (Indeed, it was precisely Langdon Gilkey's point in *Catholicism Confronts Modernity* that Catholics might profit greatly from the Protestant experience.[1])

But there are Roman Catholic examples as well.

Scripture-sharing groups have brought alive the Council's emphasis on biblical revelation. Prayer groups enrich people's lives with a whole new style of spirituality. Programs of adult and family education and theologial reflection have helped many individuals and families to integrate their personal faith with new directions in Church thought and teaching. Liturgical teams, musicians, and artists have created centers of worship in which the new rites for the Eucharist and other sacraments become genuine celebrations.

But despite these examples of successful renewal the preceding general analysis remains both important and helpful. It is important because, as encouraging as these success stories are, they remain exceptions to the general quality of parish life.

For one thing, we have found that reforms can be introduced more easily and quickly than renewal itself. Parishes everywhere, for example, have succeeded in including laity in ministry in order to relieve a shortage

of available clergy, but have not yet succeeded in install-
ing a deep-rooted sense of the laity's call to ministry
among their congregations.

For another thing, much of the work of the interior
renewal of parishioners has been done not in parish
settings or programs but by renewal "movements" such
as Cursillo, Marriage Encounter, the Charismatic
Renewal, TEC, HEC, and Search. Such programs meet
directly the challenge of preparing people for renewal
by bringing people to the point where they want
renewal, both for themselves and for their parishes.
Unfortunately these movements cannot change the parish settings to which their participants must return and
relate on a week-to-week basis. Only recently have
renewal programs developed (such as the *Renew* program in Newark or the Paulist Project in Boston) that
aim both to make people want renewal and to do
renewal on-site as a parish program. Our observation is
that until such parish-based renewal work is widespread,
the implementation of reforms will continue to run
ahead of people's readiness for renewal. For no matter
how many individuals are reached by renewal movements, the Council's agenda remains unfinished until
renewal reaches the parish as a whole. As Krister
Stendahl has said of pastoral change in general, "If it
has not yet happened in the churches, then it has not
happened yet."[2]

We believe that the analysis we offer is helpful
because it allows us to focus both on the need to complete the agenda of Vatican II and on the key factor that
will determine whether renewal catches up with reform
on the parish level: the quality of local leadership. We
have found that in any pastoral setting readiness for
renewal depends largely on the presence of leaders who
want to make renewal happen and whose style enables
them to promote it effectively.

Chapter 3

Local Leadership:
The Key to Renewal

The future of parish renewal and the ability of parishes to meet the challenge of Vatican II's unfinished agenda will depend on the renewal of local leadership. Our work has uncovered three reasons that lead us to make this assertion. First, only local pastoral leadership can assume the responsibility for finishing the Council's agenda; these leaders are the key actors in renewal. Second, so far, local leadership has been more successful in implementing reforms than in preparing people for renewal. Third, local leaders (especially clergy) have therefore experienced the same difficulties with renewal—the same delusion, disillusion, and denial—as everybody else, so that the renewal of leaders has become the precondition for their effectiveness in leading the renewal of the rest of the people. Each of these reasons deserves more detailed explanation.

After the Council it was inevitable that local leadership—specifically, local clergy—would be assigned the difficult task of making renewal happen in parishes. Who else, after all, could have been given such responsibility? The image of Catholicism as a highly centralized, monolithic structure in which pope and bishops control developments in the local parish is a myth helpful only to anti-Catholics or the invincibly ignorant. The real power behind Catholic parish life is the local clergy, and especially the local pastor. No bishop can consistently influence parish events without the support and initiative of the pastor, but the pastor may well act to direct parish life on his own, sometimes without a bishop's approval, sometimes with a bishop's active disapproval. However much Rome, or the National Council of Catholic Bishops, or any given bishop or diocese may attempt to direct the thrust or pace of reforms, anyone at all acquainted with the diversity of parish life knows that the specific course of reform and renewal in any parish is determined at the level of rectory policy.

When the task of making renewal happen fell inevitably on the shoulders of local clergy, it proved an extremely complicated undertaking that involved several things at once.

It involved implementing (or not implementing) the changes themselves, according to guidelines usually set by "higher authorities."

It involved dealing with the pastoral effects of those changes: responding to those who resisted the pace of change (whether conservatives who wished the pace were slower or progressives who wanted to speed it up) and ministering to those who, apart from their resistance or acceptance, found themselves confused, disoriented, or alienated by the effects of change.

It involved dealing with the challenge of change within leadership itself: the advent of lay ministry and leadership by parishioners, and also the twin personnel threats of the decline in priestly vocations and the emergence of religious and laity as professional leaders.

Such a complex undertaking would have been difficult even for leaders well prepared for their responsibilities. As it was, local clergy generally proceeded with renewal by placing the relatively mechanical task of implementing reforms ahead of the infinitely more delicate process of preparing people for renewal. This is not to fault clergy. How could they have done otherwise? How could local clergy prepare parishioners beforehand for the renewal to come when clergy themselves were not prepared? Specifically, priests would have needed personal preparation in advance of the changes, as well as advanced training in preparing others for change. But priests never learned this in seminary—indeed, most still do not—nor was their training updated later in their careers.

It is true that some seminaries have integrated training for leadership in renewal (often under the heading of pastoral development) into their curricula; some programs of continuing education for clergy now offer such training; and some special degree programs aim specifically at such leadership training. But the professional practice of the last two generations of clergy remains rooted in traditional seminary training.

Such seminary training for parish leadership made two assumptions. It assumed that parish life was static, with a routine determined largely by the cyclic character of the liturgical calendar, so that every year followed as the previous year. It also assumed that parish life was standardized, so that the basic rhythms, dimensions, and demands of parish life would not vary much from one parish to the next. Implicit in such training was the expectation that priests would perform their functions according to a fairly routine and predictable pattern of professional performance. Such training prepared priests to exercise leadership as institutional maintenance rather than as community development, the sort of leadership renewal would require.

When institutional maintenance is the main aim of leadership, the chief criterion of effective leadership is stability. The work of such leadership naturally centers, therefore, on two kinds of tasks: (1) routine tasks, since they are the foundation of any organization's stability, and (2) crisis management, since crises threaten stability and must be dealt with in order to restore it. In pastoral leadership the routine tasks generally occur within the framework of the liturgical year, and crisis may consist of any development that does not fit that framework— including pastoral innovations aimed at renewal.

When community development is the main aim of leadership, the chief criterion of effective leadership is responsiveness to needs. Such leadership must still perform routine tasks and deal with crises, but assumes the addition of a third priority: planning. Such leadership, knowing that community development requires change and growth, naturally centers its efforts on attempts to direct such change by a process of planning that will assure, not stability, but development based on the needs of the community.

These two approaches to parish leadership are quite incompatible in practice; if renewal required the new approach, this requirement implied that the old approach—in which most priests were trained—could not survive.

In other words, the reforms of the Council aimed to give rebirth to churches via the death of a previous style of parish life. Thus many priests, when given the job of administering these reforms, found that they were destroying the very parish system they were trained to manage, while creating a new form of parish life that they had never been prepared to direct.

A typical example comes from a priest who first became a pastor in 1967. He recalls that, after fifteen years of service to pastors who guided parishes in the pre-Conciliar mode, he found himself placed in charge of a parish system that, because of the rapid changes, bore little resemblance to his previous experience. Neither seminary training nor on-the-job learning had prepared him for this, so he began as pastor to learn a new role from scratch by sheer trial and error. The only preparation he recalls is the friendly warning offered by a *peritus* returning from the Council: "You won't recognize the Church when this is over."

Precisely because clergy were no better prepared for renewal than anyone else, it was inevitable that in their leadership roles they would experience the same difficulties with renewal as everyone else: namely, a process of implementation not preceded by preparation, resulting in the delusion that reforms equal renewal, disillusionment with the progress of renewal, and a denial of the value of further renewal.

Within the last twenty years, laity have often blamed local clergy for their role in renewal. Progressive lay people faulted clergy for ineffectiveness in promoting renewal, while conservatives faulted them for promoting it at all.

Many clergy, uncomfortable targets caught in the crossfire, shied away from renewal or even left the priesthood. Such blaming was understandable, since many laity felt victimized by the turmoil which came in the wake of the Council. But laity were generally unfair in blaming clergy, since clergy themselves were victims of renewal. Our experience in parish renewal work, in fact, has led us to conclude that we ought to view local clergy as renewal's most powerful victims.

They are powerful because despite all the changes they remain most consistently the key decision makers in parish life; their effectiveness as leaders can greatly increase the likelihood that renewal will succeed; their ineffectiveness as leaders or their active resistance to renewal can ensure renewal's delay, even its failure.

They are victims because of the circumstances imposed by the renewal process itself. They have been assigned responsibilities for making renewal happen without receiving the support and direction needed to fulfill those responsibilities. Many of our clergy are still uncomfortable with, or even unequipped for, the responsibilities of managing a renewal process with all its complexities, threats, and difficulties.

I must emphasize not only that local clergy have been victims of circumstance but also that those circumstances have not been of their own making. It must be said in defense of the ordinary, hardworking parish priest that (1) he had little or no control over the thrust of his own training, particularly if he finished seminary before 1965; (2) he had no way of foreseeing how Vatican II would radically alter the focus and criteria of effective parish leadership; (3) he had no input regarding the process for implementing renewal, nor did he volunteer for the role he was assigned in that process; (4) he was not often offered the training and supervision that would have enabled him to respond to this new role more easily.

Because clergy are both powerful and victims, they are capable of creating great harm without intending it. And as long as clergy are themselves victimized by a process that implements reforms without preparing them for renewal, their ability to exercise a leadership that can go beyond reforms and make renewal happen will be severely crippled.

So the leadership of clergy is at the heart of our crisis in renewal. Preparation and integration may be coming like the horse after the cart, but clergy will still be key people both in preparing others and in modeling the process of preparation and integration. This will be possible only to the extent that leaders themselves experience change as a renewing process. As a precondition for the renewal of others, leaders (especially clergy, but also lay and religious professionals and volunteers) must get beyond superficial reforms to a renewal of the heart of leadership.

This is not to suggest that clergy have resisted change. On the contrary, clergy have struggled with changes within leadership as much as—perhaps more than—with any other area of pastoral change. But because their approach to renewal in general has focused on reforms, their struggles to change their own leadership have displayed the same tendency and led to the same difficulties. In our work we have observed a wide range of attempts to renew leadership that, on closer examination, prove to be limited to relatively superficial reforms.

Chapter 4

The Reform of Leadership:
The Struggle Over Superficial Change

From the Council until now, changes within local leadership have focused on three reforms: (1) the use of new labels, (2) the development of new structures, and (3) the introduction of new personnel. Before analyzing these developments in parishes, however, it is worth noting that they often took their lead from similar developments in religious communities—especially women's communities, which pursued leadership reform faster and more systematically.

Among professional leadership, the use of new labels has resulted from a combination of trial and error on one hand and diocesan policies on the other. In many places, the earliest reform came when the title *curate* was dropped, often to be replaced by *associate pastor,* or later (especially when religious and laity joined staffs) by *pastoral associate.* New labels also emerged to name the professional leadership as a group: first, *rectory staff* for the priests; then, *parish staff* or *pastoral staff* to include religious and laity. Later, *team, team ministry,* and *pastoral team* came into use. In some usages the term *pastor* survived, while in others the chief priest became a team or staff member.

Among lay people, changes in titles were less visible at first. Sunday school teachers became *CCD* teachers, then *catechists.* Much of the parish work performed by volunteers gradually acquired the label *lay ministry.*

Technically this was preceded by the term *lay apostolate*, but that term was rarely used in practice, so *ministry* seemed to refer to a new reality.

Along with these formal name changes went more informal shifts, such as the tendency to address clergy and religious by first names rather than by titles and the growing prevalence of street dress among priests and especially nuns.

The development of new structures for local leadership has been, if anything, even more prominent. In many rectories priests formed staffs holding regular meetings to conduct business together. Many parish organizations and programs, previously directed by priests or sisters or lay offices, formed committees to direct their business; as many of the pre-Conciliar organizations declined, committee leadership was a consistent pattern for the newer organizations that succeeded them. Finally, the Council's mandate for the formation of parish councils found expression in a wide variety of structures, ranging from executive committees of half a dozen laity and clergy to legislative bodies of over fifty parishioners and professionals. Some structural developments provoked another wave of new labels, so that succeeding generations of parish councils were called *parish assembly, parish advisory board,* or *parish consensus committee.* Now the newly revised Code of Canon Law singles out another new structure as essential to parish operations. Ironically the structure required by the Code is not the parish council but the finance commission.

The introduction of new personnel began with the Council still in session, when lay lectors were introduced at parish masses in the early 1960s. For lay parishioners this access to what for them were new roles continued expanding to include access to sacramental preparation programs, service as eucharistic ministers, visitation workers, members of parish councils and committees.

For professional leadership, the biggest change was the inclusion of nonclergy (first religious, then laity) such as principals, DREs, liturgy coordinators, outreach workers, and others on parish staffs and teams. Thus, by the middle 1970s it was possible in nearly any diocese to find staffs that included clergy, religious, and lay professionals working together.

None of these reforms is without value. The use of new labels, for example, provides new names for the realities of Church life, some of which really are new. In some cases, leaders found that with new titles came new roles. Certainly the use of formal titles makes some practical difference. If pastoral leaders are no longer called *pastor* or if clergy are addressed by first names, this may reflect important changes in attitudes and perceptions of leaders and parish members. To call other priests *associates* rather than *curates* may reflect a willingness to view them as more than subordinates. New names for councils, committees, organizations, and programs may reflect an openness to new understanding of what they are about. And the very act of assigning new names is, of course, an exercise of power that can enable people to own the process they are undergoing.

New structures can also make a difference. The formation of staffs and teams exhibits a desire to approach leadership corporately. Parish councils give visible witness to the importance of lay leadership. New structures of any kind provide a framework, a context within which real renewal can occur; quite possibly renewal is impossible without such structures, especially if previous structures were incompatible with the kind of ministry and leadership that a renewing parish needs.

Finally, changes in personnel can make a difference as well. New blood is a common condition for organizational development, especially in occupations as stressful as pastoral ministry. In a period of transition as revolutionary as ours, the influx of religious and lay professionals and volunteers can add valuable experience and perspective to the established leadership of clergy.

But the fact remains that these leadership reforms, like Church reforms generally, have transformed the face of leadership but not its heart. Such reforms may promote the true renewal that leadership needs; but they do not constitute the renewal of leadership and may even impede it. New labels can block renewal if they refer to the same old reality and thus serve merely to hide the fact that no substantive change has occurred. New structures lead only to disillusionment if they inherit the same bad habits, dynamics, and priorities that made previous structures problematic: For example, progressive teams can be as authoritarian as any conservative pastor. Renewal gains nothing, and may be blocked, if the introduction of new personnel means merely that new faces inhabit the same old roles.

In short, the implementation of leadership reforms by unprepared leaders has often yielded superficial results that may distort the Council's intention, and—as we saw with the work of renewal in general—this is almost worse than no change at all. New names for old realities, new structures for old functions, new faces for old roles—all these may give the appearance of renewal, legitimating claims that the Council's spirit has been heeded while supporting an inadequate status quo.

No matter who the leaders are, no matter what structures they work in, no matter what label those structures bear, we still risk permanently establishing a leadership that is reformed but unrenewed until and unless we recognize that the leadership principles embraced by the Council (such as collegiality and coresponsibility) go deeper than new labels, structures, and faces. To avoid such a costly error, we must address the way leaders behave toward and relate to one another and those whom they serve. Leadership renewal, in a word, requires change in the very interior of the leaders themselves, which is then made evident by their public behavior. Such public behavior we call "style."

Chapter 5

Renewing Leadership Style: A Journey Without Maps?

In using a word like *style* to refer to the fundamental change that will enable leadership and Church life generally to get beyond mere reform to real renewal, we face the difficulty that style often refers to something rather trivial. Often people use *style* to refer only to the surface appearance of something. We say, for instance, that a person is "all style, no substance." The term *style* may also mean *fashion,* something that comes and goes according to passing preferences and tastes, in contrast to any stable or basic reality. Finally, *style* is often used to mean *image,* especially the image created by the way someone presents himself or herself in public (a politician's campaign *style,* for example), as opposed to that person's real personality and character.

In contrast to these uses of *style,* this book employs the word to name the way leaders actually behave in their leadership roles; thus *style* refers to the complex and varying patterns of behavior and relationship among ministerial leaders and between those leaders and other people. Now such patterns may incorporate some image building and may also reflect certain fashions or mannerisms. But in our view the way leaders behave, the way they present themselves to and relate with people (whether themselves, other leaders, or those they serve) will reveal who they really are as people, as ministers, and as leaders.

Paradoxically, this means that leadership style in our sense is not opposed to the substance of leadership renewal; in fact, style *is* the substance of leadership renewal. It is the stuff that really needs changing. In theological terms, we might even say that style is the sign of leadership. For leadership style is the one external public reality we can point to that reveals the presence or absence of change within leaders. Leaders may adopt new labels, develop new structures, or introduce new faces for a variety of (often quite superficial) reasons. But they do not change their consistent patterns of behavior and relationship unless and until they themselves have been changed. Once we observe such a change in style, we may conclude that some interior change also must have occurred.

With this notion of style in mind I should quickly emphasize that I am not implying that the need for change in leadership style has been totally neglected until now. As noted above, there are many success stories in the general field of pastoral renewal, though I have argued they remain exceptions to the general rule of superficial reform. The same is true in the more specialized area of leadership. The renewal movements mentioned earlier have helped many pastoral leaders to renew themselves and their styles. Also, creative communities and parishes have been experimenting with new styles of leadership for some time, and many religious communities (especially communities of women religious) have made real progress in renewing their leadership. In our work with such communities as well as with campus chaplaincies, parish staffs, parish councils, and others, we have witnessed such experiments in action. Furthermore, what is now common only in some parts of North America soon may become widespread, for we are convinced that in coming years a growing number of parishes, staffs, and communities everywhere will embark on a journey toward leadership

styles that can relate the leadership responsiblities of
pastors, staffs, religious, and laity in a way that is new,
workable, and enables the rest of renewal to proceed.

But much of the progress we have witnessed has come
only via the trial and error of creative leaders who were
courageous enough to explore uncharted waters. Our
further experience has been that for many groups such
uncharted exploration would consume too much time
or energy or resources—or else it is simply too frighten-
ing to try. These groups need guidelines marking their
way to a new style. We have come to believe that, for
the vast majority of pastoral leaders, the search for
renewed leadership style need not be—should not be—
a journey without maps.

The experiments already tried should provide valuable pointers for those just getting under way, and this
book has been written in the hope that this experience
can be presented in a way that charts a general route
that others can follow. Moreover, we believe that this
presentation can also make use of the difficulties caused
by the overemphasis on superficial change I have ana-
lyzed. To be specific, the next five chapters will distill
our experiences with leaders searching for renewal into
a model for analyzing leadership styles in a way that is at
once simple, flexible, and comprehensive. We have
found that this model can provide pastoral leaders with
a clear and adaptable map for their own particular journey toward leadership renewal.

Part II

The Four Basic Types
of Pastoral Leadership

Chapter 6

The Notion of *Recipe* in Pastoral Leadership

In our work as consultants and trainers to a wide variety of pastoral leaders over the past several years, we have made a key discovery that provides the basis for the model of leadership styles presented in the following four chapters.

We have discovered a basic paradox at work among pastoral leaders. In setting after setting we have found that each leadership group has developed its own unique style of leadership. Its style, which is not exactly like anyone else's, develops in response to a number of factors: the personalities of the leaders, the character of the population being served, the history of the setting, etc. These factors form a unique equation so that one hundred different settings could well be expected to manifest one hundred different, unique styles.

At the same time, we have also found that each of these unique styles can be understood as a *recipe* for leadership put together using four basic ingredients: obedience, division, delegation, and joint performance. Although the recipes themselves are unique, the basic ingredients are the same in setting after setting.

In each setting the way these four basic ingredients are combined determines the leadership style by forming a pattern of behavior that characterizes the way the leaders in that setting relate to themselves, each other, and those they serve. Generally one of these ingredients is dominant, and the others are combined with it in lesser proportions.

For purposes of analysis, we have taken our experience of such recipes for leadership style, boiled it down, clarified it, and purified it to distill the four ingredients into four basic *types* of pastoral leadership. We will be describing each type in its pure form, as if it were not part of a mix at all but were being practiced in isolation. Thus each type will be described as it would appear if someone followed that type one hundred percent of the time.

What the next four chapters present, then, is a set of ideal types for pastoral leadership. They are not ideal because we think they are better than others, but because they exist only as ideals; in practice they don't exist as separate realities at all. We seldom expect to find any of these types operating in its pure form, undiluted by combination with the other types. For purposes of understanding, however, it is helpful to separate them so that we can understand our own experience of leadership in terms of how these four types combine and interact.

In short, the four basic types presented in the following chapters are abstractions, not descriptions of reality. These abstractions allow us to analyze the experience of pastoral leadership in a form that is highly oversimplified, because the experience itself is too complex to analyze directly.

Each of these types represents both a different ideal of what it means to be a leader and also a different ideal of how leaders behave. In theory these ideals are quite different from one another, to the point of being logically contradictory. In practice, however, we discovered that they complement one another in most settings. Time and time again we observed leaders employing, not one style, but two or more in combination. The notion *recipe* helps us keep in mind that each type is but one ingredient for leadership and that leaders' practice will be a mix of two or more such ingredients.

The four types have emerged in a rough chronological sequence, but they do not seem to be replacing one another in any clear-cut succession. Rather, they generally accumulate, overlap, and combine. Moreover, the fourth ideal, basic type may not be the last. The point is that new ideals of leadership are emerging, and these provide an accumulation and expansion of the horizons and options for leadership style by offering leaders several options at once.

Thus, within the last generation, the framework for leadership style has become increasingly pluralized. As with any pluralism, one's ability to capitalize on the available options depends on one's ability to name, assess, and integrate them in an appropriate, consistent, and deliberate way.

Several motives underlie our presentation of these four basic types. The first is to show in some recognizable form the evidence that leadership renewal is in fact taking place. Our second motive is to identify what that renewal is, so that leaders can prepare for its coming. Our third motive is to help leaders implement their own renewed style—not by sheer trial and error, but deliberately and intentionally and consistently.

These motives are quite important to us. We have worked with many leaders whose style is undergoing renewal or is already renewed. But usually this renewal has happened more or less by accident, by the force of circumstances rather than by conscious decision. When this happens, leaders are often unaware of what they have done to accomplish their renewal. Therefore, they do not benefit from the encouragement, moral support, hope, and witness that could have been theirs had they been conscious of their own accomplishment. Such unawareness reduces those leaders' ability to enable others—especially those in parish communities struggling to get beyond mere reform—to grow as they have grown. In short, leaders should be conscious of their success so that they can model it to others. Again, when styles are changed unconsciously, new styles often are not applied consistently; so variations in style from one situation to another form an uneven, unpredictable pattern. This situational variation can block the stable, reliable patterns that make leadership dependable and therefore effective.

When presenting these four basic types to leaders, we have encountered two different responses. First, since many leaders have not yet gone beyond reform, they have found the model an exciting discovery—a useful map—that encouraged them to begin their journey toward renewal. Other leaders, having experimented on their own already, have found that the model gave form and structure to their experience and enabled them to understand and communicate better what had been happening to them. The model helped them to assess how far they have come, to overcome the frustration felt during their struggle, and to encourage and focus further efforts. Thus for both groups of leaders, the model has been an important instrument in preparing for and integrating the basic changes which leadership renewal requires.

The chapters that follow present the four basic types of leadership style, each considered separately. I would like to conclude this preliminary chapter with some remarks about the four basic types considered together.

First, as I noted in discussing the combination of several types into a leadership recipe, the major renewal of leadership is coming, not in a shift from one style to another, but in the new openness of leaders to a variety of styles (appropriate to a variety of pastoral responsibil-ities). This openness reflects leaders' awareness of the complexity of church life undergoing renewal; it also reflects leaders' recognition that effective leadership can seldom employ one kind of behavior all of the time.

Second, this openness also means that the renewal of leadership style is not a matter of choosing one type of style and excluding all the others (although one type may well predominate). Rather, renewal in style requires combining two or more of the basic types into some consistent pattern, which then forms the distinc-tive and unique style of a particular leader or leadership group.

Third, the four basic types of leadership style do not simply represent four choices but represent a complex range of choices that probably involves selecting one type as a dominant ingredient and deciding which other type(s) to include in one's recipe and in what proportion.

Finally, since each of the four basic types represents an ideal of what leadership means and how leaders behave, and since we have found that actual styles are combinations of these ideals, we should not expect to find just one of these basic types working in pure isola-tion from all the others. Such a pure type probably exists only in our presentation itself. Thus, if the description of any basic type in our model seems extreme, it is because we are describing a pure ideal that probably is never achieved. Nonetheless, these ideals are at work as ingredients in the very imperfect behav-ior of all ministerial leaders.

Leaders will probably recognize something of their behavior in each type, but no one type will describe all their behavior. Thus the key question for leaders is not, "Which type is, or should be, ours?" but rather, "How should we combine these types in building the recipe for a leadership style that makes us both more comfortable and more effective?" We will address that building process in the book's final section.

Chapter 7

The Sovereign Style

The Term *Sovereign*

We would like to describe sovereign style of leadership first, not because it is any better or worse than the three other basic styles, but simply because it is historically the earliest. Sovereign style probably predominated in most pastoral settings before the Second Vatican Council. In fact, if there are any instances where a single basic type exists in pure, undiluted form, rather than in combination with other basic types, it is either in cases of pastoral leadership before the Council, or in cases of parish or other pastoral settings where the sovereign style continued beyond 1965. In subsequent chapters we will be presenting the other basic types, not in an order of preference or value, but in the approximate chronological order in which they emerged as popular or common styles.

Another point should be made here. Although the term *sovereign* may have a negative connotation, we intend it to be understood as a neutral term. Many people think of *sovereign* as equivalent to *monarch* or even *authoritarian,* but in fact our notion in American life is that sovereignty is a good thing and may take many forms. Americans have always thought of themselves as a sovereign people—hardly a negative notion.

Sovereignty simply denotes the existence and location of supreme authority in any structure. The sovereign style of leadership, then, derives its name from the fact that it is most easily identified by the authority structure that underlies its practice.

An Illustration

An example of sovereign style might be found (as already suggested) in the traditional Roman Catholic parish leadership system, structured around the pastor and his subordinates, generally other priests.

Usually this system distinguished the pastor from his subordinates in several ways beyond the title. For one thing, the pastor was usually the oldest and was senior in point of service as well. None of the other priests had been pastor previously, but they anticipated becoming pastors later in their careers. Newly ordained clergy knew that they would have to wait a certain number of years (as many as twenty-five years in the largest dioceses) before becoming pastor and that the remainder of their priestly careers would be spent as pastor. The pastor himself, having arrived at that point in his own career already, would never again be a subordinate within the parish system.

Generally the pastor had special prerogatives and privileges that, though not part of his professional leadership, supported it: He sat at the head of the table at meals, received the most luxurious living quarters, exercised first choice over days off and vacations, and often controlled domestic management down to the choice of menus. He was the father figure in a system centered on him.

Underlying Ideals

The ideals underlying sovereign style reflect a particular image of effective leadership.

The first dimension of this image is a style of leadership that embodies order in Church life. Certainly the centralization of all authority in a single person or group, although it limits delegation, does provide a sense of order often expressed in the conviction that someone (i.e., some *one*) must be at the head of the authority structure. In this view, leadership requires a single face.

The ideal of obedience is equally important here. Not only does sovereign style suppose a single order wherein all authority flows from a single source, but the flow itself is also supposed as a system of obedience. In the case of diocesan clergy, of course, obedience is not a formal vow, yet it is a clear norm for behavior in sovereign style.

One priest was approached on this topic by a lay person who observed, "You seem to spend the first half of your career taking orders so that you can spend the second half giving them." The lay person quickly qualified his remark by noting, "But this is probably oversimplifying." The priest immediately replied, "Not at all! That's exactly what happens."

The whole division of labor in sovereign style depends on an order that results when centralized authority is always obeyed. In this view, church life goes best when each person understands one's duties as specific obligations of obedience to a single person.

Related to obedience is a third ideal, clear accountability. Because authority is indivisible, and because order and obedience are so prominent, the priests in our illustration know very well that whether they fail or succeed, they will have to answer to the pastor regarding their results.

It is not uncommon in rectories and parishes to find people referring to (though not actually addressing) the pastor as The Boss. Some pastors, more conscious than others of their reliance on sovereign style, may even proclaim, "I'm the boss," or "I enjoy being the boss."

In other systems where sovereign style dominates, it is also characteristic that people know where accountability lies. Most workers in North American society, for example, know clearly who their boss is and know exactly what account their boss expects of their work.

A final ideal underlying the use of the sovereign style is uniformity. Along with the clear sense of order, obedience, and accountability, there usually comes the expectation that the exercise of leadership authority will not vary from one task to the next, from one moment to the next, and even from one setting (e.g., parish) to the next.

So a pastor exercising sovereign style will expect to employ the same behavior pattern, whether dealing with his priests concerning parish policy, with his parishioners over personal difficulties, or with parish committees concerning specific events or plans. He will also expect that this single pattern will be found in the leadership exercised by any other authority and that it will apply as well to his own behavior in any subsequent parish where he is pastor. Leadership, in short, is conceived as a single behavior pattern that, once molded, is universally effective and therefore unchanging.

Sovereign style thus standardizes the practice of leadership to the point where *leader* conjures up a specific, uniform image: the person in a position of superior authority, identified by a special title, accorded special privilege in formal settings and deferred to in other settings, who is usually kept at a distance from others and who is expected to be decisive, firm and in charge, taking all responsibility and authority on himself or herself. This sovereign concept of leadership is both powerful and pervasive. The predominance of the sovereign style before the Council was so widespread, and its residual power remains so pervasive, that even now for many Catholics, the word *leadership* has no other meaning.

Characteristic Features

The chief feature that typifies sovereign style as a basic type is that authority is indivisible. This could mean that all authority is vested in a single group, but usually it has meant that all authority is vested a single individual (in our illustration, the pastor). In any case, the authority itself cannot be shared or divided with anyone else.

A second major feature of sovereign style is that its decision making is highly centralized. Real delegation is, if not unknown, at least uncommon; in most instances where sovereign style predominates in the leadership recipe, real delegation is in fact quite rare.

What is real delegation? It requires that the person in authority share two things with his or her subordinates: (1) the responsibility to carry out some particular tasks, projects, or activities; (2) the authority required to accomplish those responsibilities.

For example, a pastor may assign one priest responsibility for a confirmation program; that priest's responsibilities include screening applicants for confirmation to determine their readiness to receive the sacrament. If real delegation applies, that priest also would have the authority necessary to complete the process: access to parish records, authority to oblige those candidates to undergo screening, even the authority to admit or exclude applicants based on his screening.

In sovereign style, what is more likely is that the priest given the screening responsibilities will nonetheless need, when decisions are required, to turn to the pastor, who then will invoke his own authority to enforce those decisions. This happens in sovereign style because the pastor delegates responsibilities but retains all authority for himself.

The rarity of real delegation in sovereign style stems directly from the first characteristic we mentioned above, the indivisibility of authority. Real delegation requires that authority be shared, and by definition this is not characteristic of sovereign style. Authority, once vested in the pastor, must remain with him.

Typical Relationships

Given its key features and underlying ideals, certain relational qualities are typical of sovereign style. First, there is an understandable emphasis on authority in relationships, so that people who work together are not likely to relate on the basis of personality, friendship, or individual styles of behavior. Rather, they relate on the basis of rank and position.

For example, in a rectory where sovereign style prevails, the dinner table will be set routinely and invariably with the pastor at the head of the table, so that his authority functions even when the priests are at leisure. This ranking often extends to the other priests, who are seated in descending rank, with the youngest priest furthest from the pastor. The point is that rank extends to social and domestic relations between leaders, and such ranking is equally pervasive at meetings, in social relationships, and even in business relations. In language, too, authority affects relationships: Subordinates refer to those in authority by title, while using first names with one another.

A second quality of relationships in sovereign style is dependence. The subordinate depends on The Boss, not only for the authority to get things done, but even for defining his or her job, which in the sovereign style is seldom formally negotiated or recorded (with a contract, for example) but is developed and changed at the discretion of the person in authority. And since one's job definition depends on that authority, so in large degree does one's sense of accomplishment, even one's self-worth.

Another relational fact of sovereign style is that peerage is rare. By peerage we mean a relationship in which people behave essentially as equals. In sovereign style, the organization of relationships according to rank and dependence tends toward a social system in which no two persons are equal. One is either the superior or the subordinate, in relation to every other individual in the system. To return to our original example, we must now admit that we oversimplified the social system of traditional Catholic rectories by describing it as consisting simply of the pastor and his subordinates. In fact, even between subordinates there are important differences of rank; an internal pecking order appears not only at the dinner table, but in work assignments as well. Typically, for example, the youngest priest receives the work no one else wants (youth work, religious education, etc.). As one acquires seniority, one is promoted within the pecking order and has more choice regarding work. It is always clear, then, who is where in terms of career development. It is not surprising in such a system that friendship (which requires peerage) among clergy is developed and sustained not between colleagues in a rectory but between seminary classmates (one's peers in school). One may be *stationed* at a rectory with one's colleagues, but one usually socializes and vacations with classmates.

A final relational quality of sovereign style is an emphasis on respect rather than trust. Because the style relies so much on authority and obedience, and because it lacks peerage, people generally are not placed in positions of personal vulnerability toward one another. Even the relations of dependence are largely due to differences in rank, not to personal needs, or openness, or risk taking. As a result, it is not important whether people trust or even like one another personally. Indeed, one's personal feelings in general toward one's colleagues are of little importance in sovereign style, where people relate not so much person-to-person as position-to-position or rank-to-rank.

Respect, however, is important. First, subordinates find obedience easy only if they respect the judgment, competence, and character of the person giving the orders. Second, superiors must at least respect the competence of subordinates to carry out assigned tasks, or orders cannot be given with the confidence that they will be carried out.

Strengths

More than any of the other basic styles, sovereign style displays strengths and weaknesses that provoke strong reactions, since few respond to sovereign style with lukewarm indifference. More commonly, people feel either firmly attached to the style or vigorously repelled by it.

Our experience has given us opportunity for an objective and balanced evaluation of sovereign style. Because of its strengths, there are situations and settings in which sovereign leadership is especially effective. Its weaknesses, on the other hand, impose severe and in some ways unique limits whenever sovereign style is the main ingredient in a leadership recipe.

One obvious, if controversial, strength of sovereign style is its ability to model the patriarchal dimension of Judeo-Christian tradition. The controversy is, of course, rooted in the contemporary (and especially feminist) discomfort with any form of patriarchy. Such discomfort leads many to doubt the significance and value of patriarchal symbols and patterns of behavior.

Nonetheless, the existence and even prominence of such symbols and patterns within the Judeo-Christian tradition is—for better or worse—both obvious and indisputable: The Jewish faith is the faith of our *fathers,* Abraham, Isaac, Jacob; Jesus teaches his disciples to pray to God as *Abba,* a child's word for *Father*; the clergy of many Christian traditions are addressed as *Father*; the chief leader of Catholicism is *Papa,* the *Holy Father*; other symbols involve parental or quasi-parental imagery (Mary is the Mother of God; Jesus—and a pastor—is shepherd of a flock).

Whenever those in leadership desire to convey their view of the significance and value of such symbol systems, sovereign style provides a ready-made pattern of behavior that mirrors the parent-child relationship, making the leader a father-figure (or, less often, a mother-figure) to whom even elders may relate with a trust and intimacy verging on the childlike. We do not advocate such leadership, but we recognize the capacity of sovereign style to make it work.

A second strength of sovereign style is its efficiency. When authority is indivisible, decision making becomes centralized so that leadership gets fast results with a minimum of operating procedures. Such efficiency is especially helpful in emergencies or in expediting matters too minor or transitory to merit more cumbersome, time-consuming deliberations.

Third, sovereign style is economical. Its efficiency of operation allows work to be accomplished with a minimum of invested time and energy. Given the limited

likely to feel that their position is threatened by leaders who insist on acting like their parents.

Secondly, if sovereign style is strong in providing control and discipline, it suffers the corresponding weakness of not providing a strong basis for decentralization or delegation. In my description of the style's basic features, I noted the rarity of real delegation, such that subordinates are often held accountable for getting something done but do not have the authority to ensure that it will be done. The danger here is that such subordinates may find themselves out on a limb, caught between the people they are responsible for serving or leading and the pastor whose authority backs up that service. An extremely simple example is the priest who, after being delegated responsibility for forming a committee, must seek the pastor's permission when the group wants to meet in the rectory dining room.

This weakness, in the ability of sovereign style to decentralize, risks two things in pastoral work: (1) the person in authority (pastor, head chaplain, etc.) may end up doing everything, with subordinates providing only supportive assistance; or (2) the pastor may repeatedly delegate responsibility without authority, so that subordinates are continually placed in awkward positions that emphasize (rather than minimize) their status.

In a highly centralized structure, or with a pastor or other authority who enjoys exercising all authority by "holding all the reins," these features can create a highly effective leadership pattern, as I noted under "strengths." But for personalities uneasy with the burden of total authority—especially in a period of transition when that burden is changing and complex rather than routine and predictable—the need for delegation may create tension in this style, since it does not favor delegation.

A third weakness relates to this same issue. For if sovereign style conveys the impression that people can rely and depend on its leadership, it may also have the effect of discouraging people from assuming any leadership responsibility on their own. Once people are encouraged to be dependent, they may choose to remain dependent even when circumstances demand more of them.

A fourth weakness corresponds to sovereign style's strength in providing a clear, public image for the role of leadership. The weakness is simply that this clear role is increasingly problematic in our society. *Leader* is now experienced by many people as a negative, elitist term. Once alienated from the term *leader*, many people no longer relate well to those in leadership positions, even ministers in leadership, and people also have great difficulty identifying themselves as potential leaders, since such identification requires them to incorporate into their self-image a role they have negative feelings about.

In the ability of sovereign style to depersonalize relations between leaders by substituting rank, there is a related, fifth weakness: Such ranking diminishes the role that peerage plays in leadership, and the fact is that in many ways contemporary culture favors peer relationships over rank. The crisis of authority in modern culture is such that any appeal to authority or rank may complicate an issue by creating additional tensions. Isaac Hecker, who founded the Paulists as the first American-based community of Catholic priests, made no mistake in identifying his Paulists with the democratic temperament of modern America because they would "prefer to suffer from the excesses of liberty rather than from the arbitrary actions of tyranny."[1] This contemporary stress on individuality and the corollary stress on peerage between leaders puts the ranking of sovereign style at a distinct disadvantage.

A final weakness, related to the previous one, is that sovereign style tends to reinforce clericalism. If we define clericalism as the institutionalized monopoly of clergy over authority and leadership in the Church, we realize two things: (1) clericalism is the most accurate term for the elite power structure that evolved within Catholicism during the period of Christendom (roughly A.D. 325 to A.D. 1875); (2) such elitism enjoys little support or relevance in contemporary North American culture. Indeed, the drive to reject clericalism is now so widespread and deep-rooted that the most consistently expressed concern of those promoting the newly emerging ministry of the laity—whether they be laity, clergy, or bishops—is that lay ministry should not develop into "a new clericalism." This frequent and highly public concern is the best evidence I know that clericalism is a phenomenon out of place with the ongoing renewal of Catholicism. And because sovereign style relies so heavily on ranking people as subordinates and superiors, it inevitably supports clericalism, whether in its historical form (clergy as elites) or in some new form (e.g., clergy plus lay professionals as elites).

This weakness cannot be rationalized by arguing that any anticlericalism amounts to a disloyal attack on clergy. Even though anticlericalism was aimed historically at clergy (e.g., in revolutionary France) and presumed that society would be better off with no clergy at all, this new attitude is opposed not to *clergy* but to *clericalism.* It aims to strengthen the influence of clergy in an age when clericalism breeds alienation rather than obedience. In fact, because sovereign style is to some degree locked into clericalism, it may have the long-term effect of weakening clergy (or anyone in authority) when employed as the main ingredient in any leadership recipe.

Chapter 8

The Parallel Style

The Term *Parallel*

Parallel style first emerged as a common type of pastoral leadership among Catholics between 1965 and 1975, in the immediate wake of the Council, especially in the behavior of ministry teams in parishes, on college campuses, and in other Church agencies. This style was already quite widespread, however, among ministers such as hospital chaplains and military chaplains and in the academic religion departments of private high schools and colleges.

The term *parallel* is borrowed from the field of child development and refers to a type of behavior characteristic of children at a certain stage in development (which usually precedes three years of age). Several children at this stage, placed together in one space with a selection of toys, will typically play by themselves rather than with each other, with as little interest in and interaction among each other as is feasible, given the limits of space and toys. Their behavior is parallel because it moves along similar lines without actually touching. The activities are similar but performed via a process of separation and isolation that is self-imposed.

Such behavior is healthy and normal for children of this age. Eventually they grow out of it into a further stage. For our concerns it is unclear whether parallel style in pastoral leadership is only a stage leading to further development or a permanent style that will remain popular even beyond the transitions resulting from Vatican II. But the style exists in the behavior of many leaders, and we have isolated it as one of our four basic types.

An Illustration

When ministry teams first began to form after the Council, a typical pattern of behavior soon developed. The team ministry of a parish, for example, would gather several people: two, three, even four priests; one or two sisters, perhaps representing school and convent; a lay person, often hired as director of religious education. There might be a pastor among the priests, but in teams of the pure parallel type it was understood that the pastor's authority applied only to relations outside the team (accountability to the diocese, or public relations with the parishioners).

Typically, such a team begins with the assumption that its membership already knows and agrees upon what work needs to be done. This work is then viewed as the single, whole responsibility of the team; this whole is next divided into pieces, much like pieces of a pie. Each team member acquires (by assignment, preference, or some other process) a piece of the pie, which is henceforth understood to be his work or her work.

As an example, the pastor might take bookkeeping, baptismal preparation, confirmation, bingo, several parish organizations, and visitation responsibility at one nursing home. A second priest might take the youth group, Scouts, another nursing home, and liturgical planning. A third priest might take the prayer group, visitation responsibility at the local hospital, and parish census. Sacramental celebrations of baptism, Eucharist, and penance would be taken by the priests collectively, then subdivided according to a set schedule. Similar subdivisions would be made ad hoc for weddings and funerals. One sister might take responsibility for the school, PTA, and athletic league. A second sister would take the convent community, a few parish organizations, and the parish library. The lay person would be responsible for all religious education outside the school, including preparation for First Eucharist and first penance. Each person would have his or her own office space and telephone.

Once this process of division is accomplished, each team member goes off to perform his or her work. The team continues to meet twice each month but only to allow each member to keep others informed and to avoid conflicts in commitments. Each team member works alone, privately tending his or her particular piece of parish life.

It is doubtful that such a pure parallel team has ever existed, but the example cited provides an accurate description of the basic type we have called parallel style. The aptness of the term should be obvious by now: Once the parish work is subdivided, the team members perform in isolation, along parallel lines, much like children engaged in parallel play.

Underlying Ideals

The most obvious ideal behind parallel style is a high value on division and isolation, which appears both as a clear and complete division and isolation of labor and also as a clear and complete division and isolation of accountability. These aspects are clearly present in our illustrative example: The whole labor of parish leadership is divided; each team member performs his or her piece of the work apart from the others; moreover, since subsequent team gatherings are merely for information sharing, it is clear that each team member is accountable not to the team or anyone else but only to himself or herself.

If division is the first, most obvious ideal underlying parallel style, the second ideal is more fundamental: an absolute value placed on personal autonomy. In our work with parish staffs and other leaders, we have noticed that, in many cases, those who practice parallel style do so (whether consciously or not) in reaction against what they view as negative qualities of sovereign style. Many priests, for example, resist or reject the dependence on authority they experienced in systems where sovereign style was dominant. They often feel that sovereign style prevented them from being their own persons, so they seek instead a style which gives them complete autonomy to control their own work in ministry. Thus parallel style implies that pastoral leadership is best performed by self-sufficient individuals who draw on their own internal resources, without depending on any one else.

It follows that a third ideal underlying parallel style is a highly developed sense of personal responsibility. In many cases, the reaction against sovereign style applies here as well, especially among priests who feel that they were unable to exercise their own personal responsibility under sovereign style but were simply carrying out the wishes of others. A sense of responsibility, a desire to accomplish something with one's ministry, is often the driving motive behind parallel behavior.

The current political climate of the United States offers an interesting analogy. Many conservatives, having experienced the "big government" of the welfare system as an oppressive authority structure that they believe eroded personal responsibility, see in their campaign to "reduce government spending" and to "get government off our backs and out of our lives" a means of encouraging greater personal responsibility. To such people, the best government is one that leaves them alone. Similarly many priests who felt that sovereign style eroded their sense of personal responsiblity are attracted to a style whose chief virtue is to ensure that they will be left alone to do their work.

The final ideal underlying parallel style is the value placed on diversity. This contrasts sharply with the sovereign ideal of uniformity. Among leaders working in parallel, the fact that people are doing different jobs or are performing similar jobs differently is regarded as a positive quality—especially if parallel style has been chosen consciously. There is no expectation here that leadership will consist of a universal and a standardized pattern of behavior that need not vary from task to task or from place to place. On the contrary, parallel style implies that pastoral leadership involves such a variety of roles, skills, and functions that a single standard for effective leadership is impossible. Indeed, in its pure form, parallelism tends toward a variety of standards that not only differ but rarely even overlap, so that they are best applied by leaders working separately, isolated from one another.

Parallel style, then, is intrinsically pluralist in the extreme. It values the diversity of gifts among leaders to a degree that excludes most grounds for common norms that could integrate their performance into a concerted plan of action. In a sense, it is more nearly accurate to say that parallel style thus idealizes not a style of leadership but a style of leaderships.

Characteristic Features

Parallel style is often heavily task-oriented. Many clergy, feeling that sovereign style drained much energy off into issues of authority and obedience, are comfortable with parallel style precisely because it allows them to focus on the work itself. Workaholics, loners, and people who are not process-oriented thus find parallel style particularly congenial to their personalities.

Real delegation is, in contrast to sovereign style, a common and even standard feature of parallel style. This is because a complete division of labor requires not only that responsibilities be divided, but that authority be divided as well. People working in parallel must perform their own tasks, but they possess whatever authority is required to support that performance.

In the pure form of parallel style, there is in fact no overall authority to coordinate the various pieces of work, since the division of accountability has delegated 100% of the authority. This division often encourages leadership to model such delegation to others, so that delegation becomes a common and widespread practice throughout all levels of parish life.

A third feature of parallel style is self-reliance. Once people are exercising leadership according to a strict division of labor, they are pretty much left to their own resources. They may share supplies, equipment, or clerical staff with other leaders, but they do not consult with or counsel others, do not share programmatic resources, do not draw on each others' experience. Since they take all responsibility for getting the work done, they can take all the credit and must shoulder all the blame for the results. Because of this characteristic stress on self-reliance, parallel style makes each leader an Atlas holding up his or her own world of responsibilities with no other visible means of support.

A fourth feature in parallel style is that it generally lacks consensus among the leaders regarding the specific goals and objectives of the pastoral work each leader is performing. This lack stands out in parallel style, though a similar lack deserved no mention in our analysis of sovereign style. For sovereign style has characteristically been dominant in Church systems that themselves were dominated by routine, so that the goals and objectives of pastoral work were already given, established by cyclic patterns that renewed the same priorities year after year. By the time parallel style began to emerge in parishes, the setting of goals and objectives was becoming increasingly important as the reforms of the Council disturbed the routines of parish life. In parallel style, each leader sets his or her own goals and objectives within the piece of work assigned to him or her, but there is little need to share common goals, except to agree that each piece of work in the pastoral pie is worth doing.

A fifth feature of parallelism, because of the separation of task performance and the lack of consensus about goals and objectives, is that there can be no joint responsibility for performing tasks. In pure parallel style, people simply do not work together, but take responsibility for performing their respective tasks according to their own private priorities and criteria.

Finally, there is (as should be obvious by now) very little interaction among leaders who work in parallel. Like parallel lines, they do not touch; like children engaged in parallel play, they have little to do with one another. Much of the time and space, in this basic type, is spent in isolation. To invoke the image of the dinner table noted in analyzing sovereign style, the typical parallel arrangement would be for people to take their own meals according to their own schedules and preferences, to the point where the table might never be occupied by more than one person at the same time. An even clearer image, not unknown in agency and academic departments, would find each leader dining from a brown bag at his or her own desk.

Typical Relationships

The most important relational fact in parallel style is that peerage does exist but it is peerage of a peculiar sort. Unlike leaders working in sovereign style, where a ranking system pervades all relationships, those working in parallel style do not occupy ranks that immediately identify them as either superior or subordinate. Rather, a kind of peerage or equality is created by the very fact of isolation. In pure parallelism, the usual "pecking order" characteristic of sovereign style breaks down simply because people are generally not in touch with one another. If one priest is managing the books, while another priest handles liturgical planning, and a lay person or sister handles religious education, there may not be much opportunity for rank to affect their work. So they effectively become peers by virtue of the absence of interaction. They are, after all, equally alone in their work and therefore equally responsible, equally self-reliant, and equally accountable. This is admittedly a strange notion of peerage, which generally presumes interaction, but some leaders clearly prefer this sort of negative peerage to the positive inequality of sovereign style.

Another relational quality closely linked to this negative peerage is independence. Far from the dependence of subordinates on superiors for assignments, job descriptions, and the authoritative support typical of sovereign style, parallel style allows workers to generate their own assignments, carry them out, and account to themselves for their work. Thus, if they relate to others at all, they do so as independent performers who need not rely on others, do not require support, and therefore not only practice but model self-sufficiency as a quality of individual persons rather than groups or systems. This is rugged individualism in pastoral garb, which others have classified with the picturesque label "Lone Ranger ministry." In this light many of the teams that emerged after the Council could more accurately be described as companies of Lone Rangers.

Yet another relational dimension of parallel style has
to do with authority. Authority is clearly not indivisible,
as it is in sovereign style, but neither is it shared, since
those working in parallel take little responsibility in
common. Rather, authority here is divided, so divided
that it appears only in bits and pieces, one person having
authority in one area of pastoral life, another having
authority in another area. In its pure form, parallel
style provides for no coordinating authority among
these different pieces.

A final relational quality is that parallel style requires
little or no trust, simply because peole who do not
depend on one another are not at risk in relation to each
other's behavior and performance. They are not counting on one another, so it matters little whether they
trust or have personal confidence in one another.

In sovereign style, feelings toward one's colleagues
mattered less than position and rank, since these latter
were the basis of interaction and relationship. In parallel style, interaction and relationship hardly exist at all,
on any basis. Like peerage, trust presumes interaction;
in parallel style, what trust there is, is limited to a negative trust that consists only in the confidence that other
leaders will attend to their work competently enough so
that one will not be bothered by requests for assistance
and also so that they will not interfere in one's own
work. Beyond this, trust is simply not a relevant issue.

Strengths

Many of the strengths and weaknesses of parallel style
flow from its characteristic feature as the rugged individualism of pastoral ministry. As individualism offers
certain strengths and weaknesses in any setting, so does
parallel style.

A first, obvious strength of parallel style is its logisti-
cal simplicity. One need only cut up the pieces of the

pie, then go to work. There is no need for complex interpersonal dynamics, detailed planning, or deep trust. In pastoral settings of any degree of complexity (schools, parishes, etc.), this style can offer the opportunity to simplify dramatically organizational tasks that might otherwise threaten to impede the work of ministry itself.

A related strength is the capacity of parallel style for departmentalization. In settings requiring specialization rather than mere simplification, departmentalization provides a distinct label for each piece of the pie, along with the appropriate skills, responsibilities, and priorities. Thus, academic settings subdivide into departments, departments subdivide into courses, and courses into sections; chaplaincies are often departmentalized along denominational lines; campus and parish ministry often subdivide work along lines of expertise (liturgy, counselling, social action, etc.). In such settings, departmentalization may be a key to operating efficiently.

A third strength is the very isolation that parallel style brings to ministry. Since those using parallel style are left alone to pursue their own tasks, their work involves a freedom that can promote personal growth, especially if autonomy, independence, and self-reliance have not been well-developed in previous pastoral experience. This may be especially true of those whose earlier ministry developed under a prevalently sovereign style.

A fourth strength, also particularly important to those chiefly experienced in sovereign style, is parallel style's effectiveness in neutralizing the problem of authority. The fact is that for many in pastoral ministry, authority is just that, a problem. This may be due to past bad experiences; to contact with authorities who abused their position or exploited their subordinates; to a deficient theology of Church and/or ministry that cannot integrate the concepts of authority, power, or

control; to cultural pressures that cause even mild exer-
cises of authority to appear oppressive; or to personality
conflicts. The reasons are many and varied. But for
those who find authority a problem, understanding
these reasons may be less urgent than finding a solution,
and parallel style offers the quickest, simplest solution
imaginable: escape. Parallel style effectively neutralizes
the problem of authority by simply eliminating the dis-
tinction between subordinate and superior. In a word,
it eliminates the problem of authority by eliminating
authority itself.

This power of parallel style to neutralize the problem
of authority may operate even in instances where the
prevailing authority structure appears to be sovereign.
Some people, for example, have worked under pastors
who espoused sovereign style but who simply were not
strong leaders and could not impose the sort of order,
obedience, and uniformity that ideally characterize sovereign style. The result was a de facto parallelism in
which the assisting ministers performed according to
their own dictates, free from any pressuring authority.
In this sense, parallel style is not only an escape from
sovereign style, but also the by-product of a weak, ineffective sovereign style.

A fifth strength lies in parallel style's diversity. By its
nature, parallel style allows no single vision to be
imposed on the work of ministry, since each leader sets
his or her own agenda and priorities. Parallel style, in
its total decentralization of both planning and
day-to-day operations, multiplies the visions that inspire
and motivate pastoral leadership. No one vision mono-
polizes, and no one's vision is suppressed.

Weaknesses

One great weakness of parallel style is the lack of communication. Parallel operations do not touch, and when

operations have no contact, the first casualty is good communications. For leaders who value freedom more than order, this may be a price worth paying; in settings where diversity is worth more than coherence, the absence of good communications may be tolerable. But for people who need to feel informed about and linked with others and others' work, the loss of communications can be a serious problem; in settings where coordination of many ministries is essential, this loss can debilitate the whole work of ministry.

Related to this weakness are two others. On a personal level, the isolation of parallel style may be a negative rather than a positive experience. Many minsters are not comfortable performing out on a limb by themselves; many don't want to act as an Atlas holding up a whole world of responsibilities with no other visible means of support. Particularly for people who are more process-oriented, or whose theology of ministry calls for collaboration, such isolation may be a serious drawback.

On a systemic level, a third weakness results. The isolation produced by parallel style makes it difficult or impossible for people to work together even if they want to, because they have already developed different priorities and criteria for performing their work. Thus, attempts at collaboration typically generate more tension than people can handle and still work effectively. Unfortunately many church or church-related systems cannot thrive without such collaboration.

On either the personal or systematic levels, then, parallel style can threaten to stifle or even burn out operations that require collaboration.

A fourth weakness is the converse of parallel style's strength in neutralizing problems of authority. For in eliminating authority via isolation, parallel style also eliminates any positive peerage—a weakness for anyone seeking, even short of collaboration, some peer relations (peer consultation, peer supervision, etc.). Even if

I prefer to work alone, I may desire occasional
work-related opportunities to turn to others for support
of various kinds. Parallel style offers no resources for
such support.

A fifth weakness is the tendency in parallel style
toward a fragmentation of the whole thrust and scope of
pastoral leadership. For if parallel style prevents anyone from imposing his or her vision for leadership on a
group, it also stifles most attempts by that group to
develop a common, integrated vision. Such integration
requires a process of common sharing and planning, a
process absent from parallel style. The risk, then, is that
the work of leadership will follow not one vision but a
whole range of visions that may grow increasingly fragmented and chaotic. The reverse could happen, of
course—leaders' visions could grow closer or even form
a common vision—but in parallel style this could happen only by accident. Those groups that find a common
outlook indispensable to their leadership must either
rely on luck or seek some alternative (or at least complement) to parallel style.

Chapter 9

The Semimutual Style

The Term *Semimutual*

Semimutual style seems to have emerged, at the very earliest in the late 1960s, but more commonly since the early 1970s as a response to some of the felt inadequacies of parallel style in dealing with certain kinds of situations. Among some teams, semimutual style has come to dominate where parallel preceded it; generally speaking, however, semimutual style is probably the emerging favorite style of pastoral leadership, succeeding directly on sovereign style in a growing number of settings.

The term *semimutual* connotes a sort of halfhearted status, neither mutual nor any clear alternative. At the risk of being unfair to this basic type as an ideal of leadership, it must be said that the style really is a kind of hybrid, at times reflecting parallel style, at other times reflecting the fourth basic type, mutual style.

An Illustration

To illustrate a system in which semimutual style might dominate, it is helpful to cite the experience of Protestant traditions where congregational authority is a strong feature. In Congregationalist Churches, for example, the relation between pastor and the church board might provide a good example of semimutual style. This relationship might also prove similar to the experience of a company executive relating to the board of directors or trustees. There are teams in Roman Catholic ministry whose practice is predominantly semimutual. Unlike the Lone Ranger teams typical of parallel style, these semimutual teams often think of themselves as practicing shared ministry, but one leader observing semimutual behavior has remarked, "That's not really *shared* ministry; it's just divvied-up ministry."

Looking at the example of a Congregationalist pastor and board, we find a system in which the pastor, as professional clergyperson leading the parish, is hired and fired by the board, which meets as often as monthly (or as seldom as annually) to review parish business and decide on future courses of action. In this system, real decision making belongs to the board itself, and the pastor's initiative is limited to attempts to persuade the board to adopt his or her proposals. The pastor's main role is to execute the board's directives and to account to it for such execution. The pastor is thus the on-line professional exercising day-to-day leadership in the parish, while the board represents a more occasional force that sets the direction and tone for parish life.

Underlying Ideals

The ideals underlying this basic type of leadership are quite similar to those of parallel style, but with several important modifications. First, as with parallel style, a clear division of labor is stressed, but this division is not as complete as it was in parallel style. There is, moreover, some joint accountability in semimutual style, whereas there was none in parallel style. There is a stress on autonomy in both styles, and there is a kind of diversity that is valued in semimutual style that nonetheless has a more coordinated and coherent quality than does the rather random diversity typical of parallel style. So the ideals of this style are similar to those of parallel style but modified, and therefore the distinctiveness of semimutual style is reflected not so much in these ideals as in the specific features that characterize it.

Characteristic Features

Typically there are two features that define the practice of semimutual style as something distinct from parallel style. The first is that, unlike parallel style, semimutual style has a consensus about goals and objectives. Such a focus on goals and objectives has been increasingly fashionable in progressive pastoral settings in the last ten years, as more and more pastoral leaders began to learn the techniques of management by objective: assessing needs, setting goals, writing objectives, planning together, and evaluating together in staffs, councils, and committees. This attempt to achieve some common view of where one is going in pastoral leadership is the clearest symptom in any pastoral system of the emergence of semimutual style.

What remains from parallel style—and forms the second key feature of semimutual style—is that there is still no joint responsibility for the actual performance of tasks. A team or staff practicing this style may get together monthly, quarterly, or annually in order to set a basic plan for their work. But when it comes down to the seasonal, monthly, weekly, or even day-to-day performance of the pastoral tasks that are specified by that plan, the staff members operate as individuals in parallel fashion.

The third essential feature of this style is that, although there may be interaction in order to facilitate consensus building around goals and objectives, this interaction is generally periodic rather than ongoing.

At its most sophisticated, semimutual style might involve weekly staff meetings at which the business of the week is reviewed and assignments are made to individual members. Such meetings thus achieve a common understanding of the work to be done, then divide it up. Interaction during the week might therefore be minimal, and most often informal and social rather than professional. This fashion of semimutual practice involving periodic interaction has become so common that we have been able to predict, in the case of clients for parish staff development, that they will be available on Fridays—since their tasks often peak on weekends, their days off are staggered throughout the early week, and only on Fridays do they spend time together as staff.

Typical Relationships

In terms of relational qualities, semimutual style exhibits an obvious peculiarity in its treatment of peerage. Recall that in parallel style there was a peerage that came from isolation. In semimutual style there are two kinds of peerage. The first is very much like the negative peerage of parallel style; it is this peerage-via-isolation that those in semimutual style experience on the job while performing specific tasks. Here they feel a respect, a dignity, and a sense of responsibility equal to others precisely because, like others, they have been left to do their own work.

A second level of peerage comes to semimutual style in the process of planning. Here, the peerage is one of mutual responsibility, of collaborating equals. It is a more positive peerage, based on a way of relating that emerges in the sharing of responsibilities. But this second level of peerage is restricted to these periodic interactions noted above. For some practicing semimutual style, this second level of peerage may in fact be quite infrequent.

Another relational characteristic regards authority. Remember that in sovereign style authority is centralized and a key feature of the style, while in parallel style authority is divided but not shared. In semimutual style authority—like peerage—operates on two levels. On one level, that of task performance, authority is divided much as it is in parallel style. On the second level of general planning, authority is shared, because it is the planning group that takes both the responsibility and the authority for setting goals and plans.

This leads to a further relational quality: a moderate level of trust. People are performing their ministry in isolation, but these are subject to the general plan of ministry and development already set by the group. Thus, although one's performance in ministry is not at risk in relation to others, one's agenda in ministry is. So, although one may find that one's performance in a particular area is not subject to question, the value of that area as a focus of concentration may be questioned or even eliminated, so that one is sent to work on other issues that are not one's own priorities. For example, a DRE may be working on an adult education component to the CCD program; the staff working in semimutual style may not hold the DRE accountable for individual performance but may at some point in their own planning alter the priority to be given to adult education. The DRE may be more or less uncomfortable with this alteration, so he or she must have some trust in his or her own ability to work with others and some trust in their sense of responsibility and loyalty to the DRE. Trust is therefore part of semimutual style in a way that is true neither of parallel style nor of sovereign style.

The final relational dimension of semimutual style is a high level of stress. This is because the interaction of this style generates a fair degree of felt risk, strong risk, and even conflicts between the players in the system. Because the interaction is periodic and the ongoing quality of semimutual style is isolation, there is not the opportunity for ongoing contact and ongoing support, which might enable one to cope easily with those tensions. If a staff, for example, gathers quarterly to set goals and has not worked together regularly, they will find that building consensus around these goals can be very difficult. Staff members are not used to making decisions together; they work from very different perspectives; the information at their disposal may be quite varied or even contradictory; they may not have enough social contact to know each other's behavior well enough to communicate at the level their planning requires. Thus, in the pure practice of semimutual style, the experience of planning together may be highly stressful, given the inadequate relational foundation upon which group members must base their work together.

Strengths

Because semimutual style is a hybrid of two other styles (as the prefix *semi* suggests), it tends to blend the other styles' characteristics in a way that neutralizes or at least moderates many of their respective strengths and weaknesses. Semimutual style thus exhibits fewer strengths and weaknesses of its own. Instead it shows a few major benefits and limits which derive from the blending process.

The first strength offered by semimutual style is its sense of balance, which is manifested in several ways. For one thing, the departmentalization noted in parallel style is greatly moderated by semimutual style, which divides labor and accountability but retains some measure of coordination and coherence. This is because the attempt to achieve consensus about goals and objectives forces people to develop, at a minimum, common terms for dealing with that whole of their ministry that transcends the parts for which each person is responsible. For another thing, the style's emphasis on such consensus introduces an openness to planning that balances the rather extreme stress on task performance that characterizes parallel style. For people who find parallel style too task-oriented or who feel too isolated by the departmentalization of parallel style, such balance may provide a work climate that is more sociable, more relaxed, and even more humane. For people used to such balance, parallelism can feel relentlessly workaholic and atomistic.

The second major strength, which contrasts more with mutual style, is the realism of semimutual style. This realism is due especially to the limited nature of the peerage required for effective semimutual performance.

As we have already seen, the peerage required by semimutual style applies mainly to the way leaders relate to each other while planning; for most leaders, such planning occupies only a small portion of their time on the job, so the extent of peer relations required for effective performance in semimutual style is actually quite modest. This means that semimutual style provides a moderate amount of coordination without requiring extensive or frequent interaction among leaders. This limited, modest investment in interaction among leaders may be the chief attraction of semimutual style in many parish settings, especially in the more complex settings. In many parishes, for example, the number and range of pastoral responsibilities tends to stretch pastoral staffs so thin and in so many directions that extensive communication and interaction may appear to be (and may be in fact) a luxury that leaders cannot afford. If such leaders nonetheless feel that they want to experience their ministry as some sort of team experience, semimutual style presents itself as a realistic option that offers substantive coordination among leaders in return for a minimal investment of time spent together.

Weaknesses

The first weakness of semimutual style is its inability to integrate planning and performance. Since planning in semimutual style is done by the leadership group, it benefits from all the advantages of teamwork: a multiplicity of views, the testing of these views against different backgrounds and experiences, the opportunity to elicit ideas, support, and advice while still developing plans, etc. But since semimutual teamwork ends with the planning process, these benefits end when individual leaders actually go out to perform their ministries. The team members may produce a plan, but they do not carry it out as a team. Several difficulties can result.

First, the individual minister may end up attempting to carry out a plan that emerges, not from his or her own agenda, but from the team's agenda. The minister in question may not really understand, appreciate, or feel prepared for the plan delegated to him or her. This can be a source of great discomfort or stress in ministry.

Secondly, there may be a mismatch between the plan and the person responsible for its completion. Since the team doesn't actually work together in ministry, it might assign tasks to the team member who works in a particular ministerial specialty simply because the team's planning calls for that task to be performed within that specialty. The team may have little or no idea whether the assigned member is really the right person for that task, but the segregation of planning (which is team-worked) from tasks (which are not team-worked) forecloses the option of assigning anyone else.

Finally, the quality of planning itself may suffer, simply because the team's integrated vision may not be applicable to segregated performance. One minister's responsibilities, for instance, could be part of an overall plan which is well suited to the overall needs of that pastoral setting. As a piece of that plan, these responsibilities may make perfect sense, but when implemented in isolation, they lose much of their sense. This is especially true of plans in which the success of one piece depends on the success of another piece over which one has no control. Imagine, for example, a director of religious education (DRE) implementing a children's sacramental program designed to build on strong parental support, while another team member attempts without success to promote the involvement of the parents in question. The DRE is caught with a problem because some ideas that looked great during the team's planning do not look as good in the hands of individual team members.

The second major weakness of semimutual style is that the sense of peerage it provides may be too feeble to meet the leader's needs. Feeble peerage is especially evident whenever the accountability required by a staff or team conflicts with the isolation experienced by an individual minister. The individual may find, for example, that the staff wants to use staff time to review his or her performance in a particular area. Because this is not a common experience, the sense of peerage may be too weak to create the experience of a peer review—with the result that the individual may feel as though he or she is being summoned to appear before people acting as superior authorities. Such a review may be essential, but the peerage needed to make it a tolerable and humane experience may be lacking.

The third major weakness of semimutual style is that the high stress characteristic of this style can promote ineffective performance in ministry itself. In other words, stress among leaders may spill over into day-to-day performance. When this happens, a minister may begin to feel that the teamwork involved in planning does more harm than good, creating stressful dynamics that distract and preoccupy them on the job, thus making their work more difficult rather than easier. At such times people may feel strongly attracted either to parallel style, which foregoes such stress-producing teamwork altogether, or to another style that offers leaders enough time together to work through whatever stresses their joint planning generates.

Many of our clients have found that at moments like this the presence of an outside party to mediate, to provide mutual support, and if necessary to referee can be invaluable, since the needed support base (including a strong sense of fairness and trust) has not been generated internally by the system itself.

Note, finally, that this weakness applies to semimutual style in its pure form. Quite possibly people using semimutual style as a main ingredient have found ways of using social and off-the-job interactions to strengthen the bonds needed to cope with the stress of planning together. Nonetheless, high stress leading to ministerial dysfunction is a typical and symptomatic difficulty in semimutual style.

Chapter 10

The Mutual Style

The Term *Mutual*

The fourth basic type of pastoral leadership we call mutual. This style is just beginning to emerge in parish staffs and other settings but finds some early precedents in a variety of pastoral settings, in team-taught courses, and in concelebrated liturgies. As with the labels for the other three basic types, the term *mutual* is used here as a technical term; it does not necessarily mean what others (e.g., James C. Fenhagen in *Mutual Ministry*) have meant by it.

An Illustration

A good illustration of mutual style in pastoral ministry might be a retreat team that works together, offering group retreats according to a weekly routine. On Wednesday and Thursday the team assembles to plan its retreat: reviewing information about the retreatants, exploring program options, deciding on a specific program for the retreat, doing the needed preparation. On Friday the team makes immediate preparations for the retreatants' arrival, welcomes them, and begins the retreat. Saturday and Sunday continue the retreat, with the team clearing away after the retreat ends Sunday afternoon. Monday and Tuesday team members are off, returning to repeat the cycle on Wednesday.

This routine is not itself mutual style; rather, there is a whole system of operational dynamics whose presence makes such a routine workable and effective. At a regular time (e.g., weekly) the team meets, discusses upcoming team business, and establishes a general consensus about how the business should be handled. Specific assignments are then agreed upon, again by consensus, and, whenever possible, assignments for specific tasks are shared among two or more team members. Sharing assignments with others outside the team is also encouraged. There are established procedures for handling assignments together, for supporting one another on the job, and for providing one another feedback and evaluation about individual and joint performance. In large measure, the team members function as interchangeable parts in the system, since they learn each other's special skills while working together. Individual personality and style are highly valued, however, and each member's performance retains a distinctive identity.

As of this writing, such teams are still fairly uncommon; more often the labels *shared ministry* or *team ministry* refer to a group operating predominantly in parallel or semimutual style. Mutual style has probably emerged since the late 1970s, in a relatively small number of pastoral settings (such as retreat ministries) in which the options provided by combining the other three basic types seemed inadequate.

Underlying Ideals

First, as our illustration suggested, there is a heavy stress on sharing in mutual style. This cuts across many aspects of pastoral leadership to include sharing authority, sharing accountability, and, perhaps most importantly, sharing labor itself.

Thus, the ideal of authority in mutual style is corporate. No one individual has authority; authority is commonly shared by everyone in the pure mutual style. Every team member, for example, would share in decision-making and even policy-making authority. The general spirit of mutual style is to give as much access to authority as possible to *anyone* involved in any process, so that participation in leadership involves the exercise of authority according to the broadest base obtainable.

Accountability is also a shared dimension of mutual style leadership. Generally the lines of accountability do not lead back to a single source but to many sources. Often this accountability is reciprocal, so that people become accountable to each other for various kinds of behavior.

Finally, and most importantly, the ideal of sharing underlying mutual style extends to the very labor of leadership in ministry. That is, it becomes an ideal of the mutual style for leaders to perform tasks not alone, but with one another, working together wherever possible. Solo performances are therefore discouraged and avoided—and in the pure exercise of mutual style, unknown.

The second ideal underlying mutual style, after sharing, is a negative one: The autonomy that was virtually absent from sovereign style, was sought so systematically in parallel style, and was still stressed in semimutual style is simply no longer valued in the emergence of mutual style. In this respect, mutual and sovereign styles resemble one another, for the independence and autonomy of the individual are not valued in either one. Leaders are judged by factors other than their ability to stand on their own.

A third ideal, namely, a new stress on integration, compensates for the lack of stress on autonomy. This ideal has three dimensions. The first is the notion that a leader will be a person who is internally integrated: well balanced, emotionally and developmentally stable. Second, this internal integration is accompanied by a corporate integration among members of the leadership group, and between them and their environment; in fact, their ongoing internal integration depends heavily on the mutual support they gain by being integrated with each other. In mutual style, then, integration is both a psychological climate and a social system. Third, integration implies that leadership should effect an integration of the various tasks of the leadership, so that they form a coherent and systematic whole.

The result of all this integration—personal, corporate, and operational—is a sort of diversified unity, which is the fourth and final ideal underlying mutual style. As an ideal it leans, on the one hand, toward the uniformity of sovereign style but also, on the other hand, toward the pluralized diversities of the parallel and semimutual styles.

Characteristic Features

The characteristic features of mutual style are, predictably, precisely those features that distinguish semimutual style from parallel. Mutual style is largely different from semimutual style because it has dropped those qualities of parallel style which semimutual style retained.

Thus, like semimutual style, mutual style features consensus among leaders about goals and objectives. But, unlike semimutual style, mutual style calls for a joint responsibility for the performance of the actual tasks envisaged by such objectives. The shared responsibility in mutual style, therefore, includes not only the preliminary task of developing a general plan for leadership in a given time period but also the subsequent tasks that implement that plan.

Another feature characteristic of mutual style is that on-the-job interaction among leaders, which was absent in parallel style and only periodically found in semimutual style, becomes an ongoing, consistent, and abiding dimension of mutual style. Indeed, it may be that, in the concrete analysis of such styles, the surest symptom of the presence (or even dominance) of mutual style is a constant interaction among the leadership.

Typical Relationships

The most obvious relational quality in mutual style is a strong sense of peerage among leaders. This sense of peerage is quite different from what is found in semimutual style not only because it is stronger, but because it is no longer the negative peerage (which originally emerged in parallel style) that comes from isolation. That sort of negative peerage depends on eliminating relationships of rank and position among leaders by eliminating interaction. In mutual style, peerage depends on the way leaders *do* interact, rather than on the fact that they don't; it is therefore a more positive peerage that denotes not the distance between individuals as the basis for their equality, but the fact that they actually come together as equals. This is perhaps the outstanding relational quality of mutual style. Leaders who practice it experience a profound equality, and even interchangeability, between themselves and other leaders.

Less obvious, yet deeper, within mutual style is the relational dimension of interdependence. Relationships within mutual style quickly and consistently become interdependent precisely because of the way leaders interact in a style where they are not just encouraged but even forced to rely upon one another. Because autonomy is not stressed, because both

accountability and labor are shared, there is a constant
need for reciprocal and mutual bonds of reliance that
make people interdependent on one another. This
means that no one person, in a system dominated by
mutual style, can perform very much of his or her leadership effectively without others' help. But each leader
knows that his or her need for others is an experience
that all the other leaders share.

Another relational quality is that authority in mutual
style exists, not on the two levels of divided and shared
found in semimutual, but almost exclusively as a shared
quality. In pure mutual style it would be rare to find one
person or subgroup exercising authority independently
of other leaders.

The final relational quality, which is actually a precondition for the ongoing practice of mutual style, is a
high level of trust among leaders. People who employ
mutual style interact so intensely, work so closely,
depend so heavily on one another, that they take enor-
mous risks. They are, in effect, counting on the other
leaders to support their own professional effectiveness,
their own personal stability, and their continued growth
and development. To count on others in this way, one
must trust implicitly the others' reliability, personal
integrity, and strength of character. Without such trust
no leader would feel comfortable being so vulnerable or
risking so much on another's performance. Without
such trust one would avoid such risk out of fear of failure or hurt. Without such trust one would probably
find it emotionally easier to perform tasks on one's own,
thus reverting to another style of leadership.

This need for trust also extends to professional trust
in the abilities and competence of other people. Since
leaders actually are sharing labor with others, they must
be convinced that relying on others is better than doing
everything by oneself. For example, if personal styles of
performance or presentation vary, a leader must trust

others in order to avoid the nagging regret that he or she would have been better off alone. Sharing the responsibility for tasks makes the results less predictable, less within one's control. Thus, sharing is always harder than going it alone; only trust can make it better as well. The surrender of one's control over the way tasks are actually performed is both characteristic of the deemphasis on personal autonomy and independence and highly linked to the level of trust.

Strengths

The strengths and weaknesses of mutual style must always be discussed with one preliminary but overriding consideration in mind: The first response of most progressive pastoral leaders to mutual style is so positive that one must often expend extraordinary efforts to make them aware of its limitations. In many quarters there is a positive bias that (rather blindly) favors mutual style over the other styles. Time after time our clients have jumped to adopt mutual style, only to realize gradually that it is not suitable for every minister in every setting. This bias may be due in part to the word *mutual*, which enjoys a good image in contemporary pastoral circles. In any case, mutual style often looks better in prospect than it turns out to be in practice. Like the other styles we have studied, mutual style cannot be expected to stand alone, meeting all ministers' needs for leadership; it too must be part of a recipe.

Nonetheless, it is quite true that mutual style offers several strengths. First among these is the obvious fact that, when exercising mutual ministry, one is never alone. The one constant in mutual style is the ongoing interaction among leaders, their continual presence to one another. Such presence can, under the right conditions, become a sustaining force that helps leaders withstand the pressures, stresses, and responsibilities of ministry. This means that mutual style can create a work environment in which the high job investment typical of most ministers is matched by the high quality of relationships that support that investment.

A second strength follows directly: Mutual style overcomes the isolation that, in one way or another, is characteristic of all the other styles. Mutual style replaces the obedience of sovereign style, the division of parallel style, and the delegation of semimutual style with a single operating principle: the joint performance of all ministry. For those tired of ministry as a solitary state of being, the attraction of such joint performance may be irresistible.

A third, related strength is the tendency in mutual style for integration to triumph over fragmentation. We have seen that mutual style aims at internal integration of individual leaders, at corporate integration among them, and at the integration of their tasks. At best, this creates a coherent and systematic approach to, and performance of, the work of ministry that contrasts markedly with the pieces of the pie we found in parallel style. When mutual style succeeds, it yields a teamwork that can acquire an almost organic unity, so that a wide and varied range of resources, skills, and gifts interlock in a complex pattern that reflects at once the richness and the wholeness of church and ministry. In a church where fragmentation and polarization have been the unfortunate but all too common by-products of renewal, this integrating power may appear not just as an attractive dimension of mutual style but as a top pastoral priority in one's whole ministry.

A fourth strength, already hinted at, is mutual style's ability to multiply the resources for ministry within a given setting. When leaders perform their minstry as a team always working together, they automatically experience an extra dimension: on-the-job learning.

This learning process begins when leaders are continually present to observe each other's performance; it continues when they attempt to expand their personal repertoires by trying out what they have observed their colleagues doing; and it concludes with the acquisition of new skills and resources for one's own performance. Teams that work together like this for several years find that each person's original specialties become contagious, so that eventually individual colleagues are capable of a much wider range of effective ministry than before. Each person will retain certain strengths and weaknesses, so colleagues will not usually become completely interchangeable. Even so, the list of each person's abilities (both strengths *and* weaknesses) will be considerably longer than at the outset. This increase in each minister's abilities means that the team as a whole has more to offer its clientele, even though the team has not added members. In settings where there is a shortage of personnel, or where needs cannot be easily compartmentalized, this multiplication of resources may be a great practical value.

A fifth (and extremely complex) strength of mutual style is that the experience of sharing which characterizes the style yields a variety of benefits. First, the sharing itself is a powerful attraction for many people in ministry. Personally, sharing removes the threat of loneliness from ministry. Professionally, sharing lightens the burdens and stresses of ministry while offering opportunities for growth and learning. Theologically, sharing makes practical sense out of notions like *people of God* and *diversity of gifts*. Culturally, sharing offers a prophetic witness against the fragmented isolation of so much of contemporary living.

Secondly, the sharing in mutual style entails a strong peerage whose root is a profound and radical equality that cuts through all distinctions of office, rank, personality, sex, and age. Such peerage gives mutual style a powerful timeliness, for the equality it reflects and promotes is arguably the most significant value of our age; yet, at the same time, such peerage retrieves the fundamental Christian notion that our common bond in Christ is stronger than all our differences.

Finally, sharing leads to the interdependence that is mutual style's deepest relational dimension, and this too has a profound resonance in our theology and culture. The U.S. Catholic bishops' document *Called and Gifted: The American Catholic Laity* noted that many laity fail to exercise in their ministry a "mature interdependence" that is already present in the rest of their lives. Our staff, responding to the bishops' request for a commentary, suggested that emerging styles of pastoral leadership might be decisive in promoting interdependence in both Church and world. We wrote:

> While lay people may be familiar with and ready for peerage, they are often less familiar with the experience of interdependence. We should explore whether their "other areas of life" really are imbued with *inter*dependence, or whether the usual alternative to dependence in today's American society is, in fact, a self-sufficient *in*dependence, which fits well with self-direction but not with collaboration or sharing. If the latter is true, then the lessons learnt in developing a mature lay ministry may imply radical benefits which go beyond ministry itself to those "other areas of life." It would be a significant achievement if the Church's struggle to develop its laity enabled it to model interdependence to a world in which mature sharing (in politics, economics, social and cultural life) is sorely needed but badly lacking.[1]

The sixth and final strength of mutual style is the freedom it offers on many levels, and especially the freedom to be human: to be imperfect, to be vulnerable, to need to rely on others even in one's ministry, to fail, to struggle and grow. Mutual style is capable of liberating the humanity in ministry because it rejects implicitly any tendency (whether psychological, emotional, theological, or institutional) to identify the minister with the divine in Christ. This contrasts most sharply with parallel style, in which the minister as Lone Ranger may be deeply tempted to become minister as Savior. The very operation of mutual style makes it clear that no minister can be self-sufficient, no minister can be Savior. This style thus encourages the minister to identify with the human Jesus as a model, thereby freeing the minister to seek increasing effectiveness without ever leaving self behind. This freedom is at once the most subtle attraction and the most profound benefit of mutual style.

Weaknesses

Because of the contemporary bias in favor of mutuality, the weaknesses of mutual style can be difficult to perceive when one is considering mutual style as an option. However, the weaknesses become quite real once one attempts to practice it. Those attracted to mutual style need to read this section with extreme care, lest the style's attraction become a blind pursuit, founded on a naive idealism and leading to frustration and disillusion.

The first weakness of mutual style is that those in mutual ministry are never alone. I have already noted this fact as a strength because it remedies the isolation many ministers suffer. But it also imposes a burden on those who practice mutual ministry: the burden of group maintenance.

Since mutual ministry requires nearly all ministry to be performed in groups of two or more, members of mutual style teams are forced to promote and sustain the conditions that make the whole team a strong foundation for personal and professional interaction. This

means (1) acquiring and learning procedures for help-
ing the group grow, develop, and respond to its own
internal dynamics; (2) setting aside the time necessary to
apply these procedures consistently (e.g., providing
time for team planning, supervision, evaluation, feedback, personal sharing and support, prayer, play, etc.);
(3) developing a balance between the time and energy
the team invests in its pastoral tasks, on the one hand,
and the time and energy it invests in the process of its
own maintenance, on the other.

These requirements constitute a weakness simply
because for many ministers, they are unrealistic: Many
people in ministry are too task-oriented to make such an
investment in group process; many others feel called to
serve those in need of their ministerial gifts, rather than
to spend time serving (and being served by) other ministers; many more are simply not prepared by their own
training and disposition to engage in such a group maintenance process, which requires both extensive group
skills and a sometimes prodigious patience with one's
colleagues. In short, mutual ministry requires an investment in service to other ministers that some people will
not want to make and others will not be able to make
even if they want to. Moreover, in some pastoral settings, such maintenance is unrealistic, whether or not
the individuals are willing or capable, simply because
their responsibilities are too time-consuming to leave
suffecent time to be together.

This last point suggests a second weakness of mutual
style: its tendency to expend a lot of human resources to
achieve its results. Because mutual style shares not only
authority and accountability but even labor, it follows
that those teams relying on mutual style cannot be
spread very thin. They cannot, for example, allow
members to split up responsibilities by performing ministries individually. By requiring that ministers perform, not solo, but at least in tandem, mutual style

commits itself to a labor-intensive use of personnel resources that in many hard-pressed pastoral settings is a luxury that leaders may desire but cannot afford. In most parishes, for example, the idea of teaming up on every pastoral activity (including liturgical celebrations) seems quite preposterous.

The third weakness—or at least problem—with mutual style lies in its centralization of authority. This centralization brings mutual style closer to sovereign style than to any other. While sovereign style vests authority in an individual (or some ruling elite), mutual style vests authority in the leadership group as a whole. For some team members, the simple fact of being included as part of the authority-structure will be enough to satisfy their personal needs for control. For others, however, especially for those already familiar with parallel and/or semimutual style, the surrender of personal autonomy and independence to the centralized authority of the group may seem just as onerous (even oppressive) as it does with sovereign style's surrender to an individual. No matter how attracted they may be to the *ideal* of mutual style, some people never become comfortable with its authority but feel a chronic unease rooted in the underlying sense that their entire performance as minister is being watched by others and that their individual private agenda are constantly subject to group approval.

The fourth weakness is that mutual style greatly complicates the process of making decisions. In both sovereign style and parallel style, key decisions are made by single individuals. In semimutual style, group decision making is limited to a restricted area of rather general issues. In mutual style, by contrast, group decision making extends to all but the most routine, trivial, or urgent issues. For most groups, this imposes a heavy burden of consensus building and clear communication.

At best, this burden is the price one pays for the broader outlook and resources of several converging perspectives. At worst, it is a time- and energy-consuming exercise that complicates the work of ministry without either enabling or illuminating it. At the very least, mutual style requires—as a precondition—a high investment in decision-by-consensus on the part of its practitioners. Otherwise, the exercise of mutual style is bound to be futile and self-defeating.

A fifth and final weakness (or at least difficulty) with mutual style is a risk which derives not so much from its intrinsic qualities as from the pastoral conditions surrounding it. Given the traditional—and contemporary —stress on sharing, community, and mutuality, mutual style may attract people who expect it to provide not only professional support but community and even friendship. This is an understandable but mortal temptation, for the fact is that the teamwork typical of mutual style is not the same thing as community or friendship. It is true that community and/or friendship may provide a foundation or context for mutual ministry, but the mutual style does not depend on such a community or friendship, nor can it be depended upon to provide community or friendship. In an age when *community* has become a watchword, the tendency to confuse community with teamwork may be unavoidable, but it must be resisted if mutual style is not to become a mirage, a mistaken promise receding into a horizon one can never reach.

Part III

Choosing a Leadership Style

Chapter 11

Accountability

Every leadership recipe is a unique way of arranging the activities of leaders in relation to themselves, each other, and their clients. This follows from the fact that the four basic leadership styles are nothing but variations on the theme, "division of labor" (recognizing, of course, that mutual style varies the theme by not dividing labor at all).

But no matter how the theme is varied, certain issues or questions must be addressed if any recipe is to be effective: How does the recipe ensure that leaders receive the help they need to be effective? (Chapter 12) How is the work of leaders to be evaluated and improved? (Chapter 13) What sort of training prepares or qualifies ministers for a given recipe? (Chapter 14)

But prior to these questions comes another: How does the recipe achieve the basic dependability of ensuring that work gets done in the first place? This is the function of accountability, which monitors neither the quality nor the results of leaders' work but its actual performance. As with the steward in the gospels called to account for his stewardship, the issue here is not "How well did things go?" or "How do you feel about your performance?" but simply "What did you do?" The specific point of this question is to determine whether whatever was expected, planned, assigned, or promised actually took place.

Our purpose here and in the following chapters is to compare and contrast the consequences of choosing any of the four basic styles as the main ingredient for one's recipe. Recall that in most recipes one style dominates; this dominance has decisive practical effects on how leaders meet their needs for accountability. One key to choosing the right recipe is to foresee how one will get the accountability one wants.

There are two basic questions to ask in determining the impact of any main ingredient on accountability. First, what is accountability about, what does one actually account for? Second, to whom is accountability given, and how? For each of the four basic leadership styles, the answers to both questions are quite distinct.

In sovereign style one is accountable for two things. First, one must be able to demonstrate obedience to authority: that one in fact carries out one's assignments. Second, accountability in sovereign style concerns one's support for the agenda of those in authority. If this agenda changes, one becomes accountable for a different kind of behavior that supports the new agenda. Thus, before Vatican II, local clergy were mainly accountable for a fairly stable routine of maintaining a well-established system of parish life, but after the Council they became rather suddenly accountable for introducing and implementing a whole series of legislated reforms in their parishes. So one may be cast in either the role of defender of the status quo or the role of change agent, but in either case the issue is the same: being accountable for supporting the agenda of superior authorities.

To whom is one accountable in sovereign style? Generally, to one's immediate superior, who, in turn, is accountable to his or her immediate superior, and so on. The obvious exception is the case of open conflict between subordinate and superior. In such cases there may be provision for the subordinate to appeal to a higher authority "over the head" of the immediate superior. For example, a parish council might appeal a pastor's decision to dissolve the council, claiming he had abused his authority. Depending on the specific institutional structure in question, such an appeal may have either a fair chance of success or no chance at all. Nevertheless such an appeal remains characteristic of the sovereign style, if only as an exception to the rule.

How does one account to one's superior? In most pastoral settings, accountability is provided through informal (usually verbal) reports. The experience may vary, because the person in authority may prefer to keep either loose or tight reins on subordinates, but the reins are always there. In fact, much of the on-the-job communication and interaction in sovereign style consists of reporting progress on assigned tasks. This happens in sovereign style because accountability replaces the function of delegation: Accountability ensures that the work gets done even though the person in authority does not do it all. Unlike delegation, accountability keeps all authority in the hands of the superior to whom others report.

In parallel style accountability in the usual sense is virtually ruled out; accountability usually denotes a kind of interaction, and parallel style tends to exclude interaction. All one may expect is a sort of accountability to *oneself*: People may set goals for themselves, even make contracts with themselves. Thus, accountability may be about almost anything. One may exclude or include anything one likes from such self-contracts, at will. But underlying any self-accountability is the burden of integrity, which in parallel style one assumes alone. After all, self-accounting makes no sense and serves no purpose unless it is based on, and promotes the development of, several personal qualities: self-honesty, self-awareness, self-discipline, self-generosity. Accountability of this kind functions less to ensure that work gets done (i.e., like delegation), than to promote one's personal growth. It is, then, not unlike the self-criticism practiced in some religious communities and Marxist cells.

Such a peculiar style of accountability may bring great benefits and might be a useful practice even within other styles. It may even be that the experience of parallel style at one point in one's career may yield the long-term benefit of a more self-accountable personal style in ministry that continues even after one has acquired a new leadership style. But this is not the sort of accountability one speaks of in the other styles, and we must remember that in parallel style there is no way to be held accountable even for self-accountability.

As with parallel style, the burden of accountability in semimutual style is largely on oneself as far as day-to-day tasks are concerned. But the joint planning typical of semimutual style introduces a major difference, for planning makes one accountable to other leaders at least periodically. In fact, a major feature of such planning may be time spent reviewing the results of previous plans, partly to evaluate their success, but partly as well to check whether the group's priorities translated into actual performance in the hands of individual leaders. Since this checking might happen no more than two or three times a year, it must remain focused on general priorities rather than specific tasks. An individual charged with conducting a confirmation program, for example, might well rely on self-accountability to ensure most of the work being done, knowing all along that others will merely need to know the general shape of the resulting program. Even so, one may find that the knowledge that such general accounting must eventually be made spurs one to be more conscientious about self-accountability along the way. Such is the logic behind the accountability procedures of many funding foundations: They may not have time to evaluate the use of their grants, but they suspect that merely asking

for a report enhances the likelihood of good performance. So too in semimutual ministry: This style leaves
day-to-day accountability to oneself but also provides
for a general accounting of one's self-accountability.

In mutual style there is no division of labor: The work
is shared, and the accountability is shared with it. Thus
accountability in mutual style, like the work itself, is
ongoing, joint, reciprocal, rather than one-way.

What is accountability about in mutual style? The
range of possible options is wide: One may be asked to
account for a single phone call or a five-year project;
about one's ministry to a single person or one's progress
with a whole constituency. In mutual style, one's tasks
are neither orders from a superior nor one's own ideas;
they are plans consented to by both oneself and one's
colleagues. And because of the consent of both self and
colleagues, one is accountable first of all to oneself, and
then to one's colleagues. Both accountings may occur
simultaneously, of course, since colleagues may be present at any time in mutual style. Furthermore, the
reciprocity of mutual style requires one not only to be
held accountable but to expect similar accounting from
others as well.

If accountability is the key to the reliability of any
division of leaders' labor, because it ensures that work,
once divided, will get done, then it follows that any
leadership recipe will need at least *some* accountability.

Each basic style provides its own kind of accountability, but, after establishing one of these styles as the main
ingredient in a leadership recipe, one may still feel that
the accountability provided by the main ingredient does
not deliver the reliability one needs. In that case, one
should add, as a minor ingredient, whatever style offers
the kind of accountability one needs most. Thus,
accountability is often one area of leadership style
where a minor ingredient is deliberately added to shape
up the reliability of a recipe whose main ingredient

seems weak on accountability. This adding process allows leaders to stress the style they want, while guaranteeing adequate checks on their own (and others') performance.

Chapter 12

Support and Supervision

In choosing a recipe for one's leadership style, one important implication to consider is the effect of one's choices on the prospects for support and supervision. This chapter explores that implication.

In our view, it is important to keep support and supervision closely linked, lest we misunderstand the practical meaning of supervision. The usual dictionary sense of *supervise* is to *oversee,* but in recent pastoral practice and theological education (especially field education) the term *supervision* refers to a process that is not so much being watched, judged, and directed from above as being guided, encouraged, and supported from below. In this sense, supervision's function is neither merely the accountability that ensures tasks have been performed (Chapter 11), nor the evaluation that assesses that performance (Chapter 13). Rather, supervision in this wider sense comes to mean a supportive function performed not only by one's superiors but perhaps also by one's peers.

In general, pastoral supervision aims to promote the personal formation and professional development and maintenance of those in ministry. In particular, such supervision entails formal or informal procedures that enable the minister to reflect on his or her experience, learn from that reflection, and employ such learning to prepare intellectually, emotionally, and psychologically for future experiences.

Supervision is a dynamic, liberating, growth-producing form of ministry which manages institutional realities in such a way that people are freed and enabled to realize their own potential and to respond to the demands and opportunities of life which a God of Creation makes possible.[1]

Not every ministry requires the same amount or kind of supervision, and different stages of ministerial development present different needs for supervision and support. Depending on these factors, one's choice of a leadership style carries implications for devising forms of support and supervision that fit one's needs. Accordingly, this chapter compares the impact of each style on support and supervision.

In sovereign style, supervision is often not given at all. The style is simply not geared toward support and supervision: The minister is given a job to do, instructed and ordered to do it, and obeys. The minister goes off, performs the assigned task, and then reports back at a later time. Not much question here of patting the minister on the back, making sure he or she got the preparation and help needed, or talking with him or her about how the work is going. Thus, sovereign style tends to promote a system in which all that matters is that one is following orders, and this controls one's performance in a way that may not require much support or supervision.

When supervision is given in sovereign style, it is often done informally. It is not as though there were specific and regular times, places, and procedures for supervision: a meeting every Friday afternoon at 3:00 P.M., for example, to discuss how the minister is doing, to help him or her feel better about the job. Rather, supervision may occur over lunch, or whenever superiors and subordinates happen upon an opportune moment.

Also, such informal supervision tends to be centered on the pastor (or other sovereign authority); it is the pastor's job to give such support. For example, it typically happens that the pastor might feel the associate needs a little encouragement and might call him into his office or room for a little chat, man-to-man (or even father to son) to cheer him up, support him, give him a pat on the back (or boot on the backside), and send him on his way hoping he will be better off.

Moreover, such supervision depends largely on the personality of the sovereign: It is performed according to the values and inclinations of the particular person who happens to occupy the position of authority. The same associate (to renew an example) may find next week that there is a new pastor, who is not the sort of man given to little chats. The associate remains within the same setting and the same leadership style, but the personalities have changed, and that makes all the difference. In short, the frequency and quality of support and supervision depend, not on standardized organizational policies, procedures, and structures that are built in and dependable, but on individual factors that are constantly subject to change within a setting and vary widely between settings.

In parallel style the case is somewhat different. For one thing, there may be little opportunity for support and supervision. Why? Because being together is a precondition for supervision, and in parallel style people are not together very much. A real giveaway is the following, fairly common occurrence: The issue of supervision or support (especially peer support) comes up, and people consult their calendars only to find that they cannot agree on a common date to get together, precisely because their general pattern is to work alone. They might be together off the job (e.g., at meals), but by definition their lines of work, because they are parallel, do not converge. In contrast, if people were working together, they would be able to provide each other with informal support and supervision during their ongoing interaction.

Beyond the lack of opportunity is a further, stronger factor that adds to the lack of support and supervision in parallel style. Parallel style gives little recognition to the *need* for support and supervision. Recall the value placed on autonomy, independence, and separation in parallel style. These ideals presume that one is ready and able to do one's work without anyone supporting or supervising. Underlying parallel style is the idea that the minister is a self-sufficient, responsible, rugged individual. Why would he or she need support? When this lack of recognition is added to the lack of opportunity, it is no surprise that in settings where parallel style dominates, the occurrence of support and supervison tends to be sporadic.

It also tends to be problematic. When support and supervision do occur in parallel style, they often surface delicate issues of turf. Often someone wants to be helpful to a colleague who appears to be struggling. So he or she offers support only to discover that the colleague is deeply threatened that his or her piece of the pie is being taken over, and further feels that this is unfair (or even implies a judgment of failure), since everyone else's piece is left alone. These reactions are quite reminiscent of children who, accustomed only to parallel play, are suddenly expected to share. Like such children, ministers working in parallel are likely to respond (or want to respond) with something like "Wait a minute! What gives you the right to interfere in my work? This is my turf. Out!"

Thus, the well-intentioned offer of support and supervision in parallel style often backfires, because the individual on the receiving end experiences not support but interference. When people rush in to help, the behavior is so out of parallel character that it promotes a sense of crisis that rarely proves constructive.

The chief difficulty with the practice of support and supervision in semimutual style is that it tends to be inconsistent. Since the interaction between people in this style is only periodic and tends to be limited to general decision making and planning, support and supervision tend to be restricted to those areas of one's work.

Thus support and supervision in semimutual style tend to address, not how things are going on a day-to-day or week-to-week basis, but only the level of one's pastoral priorities: general goals, objectives, and agenda. One's actual experience of performing ministry, which happens in isolation, generally gets left out. The result is a sense of inconsistency due to the feeling that one can rely on other's help in making plans but not in carrying them out. A case in point is the DRE who receives welcome staff support, input, and encouragement regarding the plans for a new confirmation program but later feels isolated and overwhelmed with the responsibility for actually coordinating the program.

Whenever mutual style is the main ingredient, support and supervision must be built in as a system, or trouble will quickly follow. The time that is required for this is one of the practical drawbacks of mutual style for pastoral staffs. Support and supervision must be ongoing and consistent. If ministers are not supporting one another consistently, it becomes very difficult to withstand the frictions that come from working together. Most of the time it is not as easy working together as it would be to work alone, and the only thing that makes it better is the fact that, when ministers are working together, they can support one another. For example, planning a weekend retreat in a group of two, three, or four may be much harder than simply planning it alone, unless ministers really experience the ability to help one another with suggestions and ideas. Even then, planning by committee may remain a difficult and time-consuming process, but the sense of support can make it better than working alone.

Second, such a system must provide both formal and informal opportunities for support and supervision. The formal opportunities might occur, for instance, during weekly staff meetings or even in separate supervisory sessions, especially when working with interns, field education students, lay ministry trainees, etc. The informal opportunities may occur on particular work occasions, when people observe their colleagues at work and offer support: "I can help you with that." "Are things going okay here?" It may also happen between work occasions as one reviews progress informally: "Are you enjoying working on that program?" "Are you looking forward to tomorrow's session?" The system must provide for supervision and support, and the people in it must practice both, or the strain of constantly working together can take its toll.

Third, support and supervision must address not only pastoral priorities and planning (goals, objectives, agenda), but also the actual performance of specific ministerial tasks. An example: A minister draws up a plan for a weekend retreat after discussion with others, and part of the plan is a list of needed supplies. But the minister is busy with other business the day before, so a colleague says, "Let's sit down and list all the supplies; then I'll get them ready." Without such support and flexibility, neither minister could be as effective. Unless one is ready to provide such support, one forfeits the togetherness offered by mutual style.

From all of the above, it might seem obvious that mutual style tends to be better at providing for support and supervision than the other three styles. Although that may be true, it is not the point of our comparisons.

The point is quite different: When we choose any leadership recipe, we need a main ingredient. Whatever main ingredient we choose, the choice will imply certain trade-offs, certain benefits, and certain sacrifices. Concerning support and supervision, the trade-offs look like this: The first three styles do not need or rely on support and supervision, but neither do they provide for it very well. If one chooses the sovereign, parallel, or semimutual as a main ingredient, support and supervision must be regarded as optional equipment. If one's ministry does not require them, any of these three styles may suit. But if one's ministry does require, or can benefit from, support and supervision, one will need to add them on deliberately, all the while recognizing that one's main ingredient does not encourage them.

If the main ingredient of one's ministry recipe is mutual style, the trade-off is quite different: Support and supervision must be regarded as part of that style's standard equipment—they are part of the package—and one must be prepared to pay the price in time and energy to make it work. In mutual style one does not have the option of foregoing support and supervision, nor, if one's ministry requires them, does one have to make plans to add them into a style that does not value them highly nor integrate them easily.

Chapter 13

Feedback and Evaluation

There are three basic reasons why persons working in ministry may need opportunities for feedback and evaluation from others. First, we all have blind spots that keep us from a completely objective perception of our own performance; only others can fill in those blind spots for us, so we must depend on their views if we want our performance to improve. Second, we may want a second opinion when we assess our own performance. What we regard as a weakness may appear a strength to others. Third, even when we are well established in a ministry, and we can perform comfortably and well, feedback and evaluation keep in our minds areas we can continue to build on (our strengths) as well as areas we might continue to work on (our weaknesses). But such opportunities for feedback and evaluation vary a great deal—as do the form and content for feedback and evaluation—depending on which basic style supplies the "main ingredient" in a minister's recipe.

If sovereign style dominates, one may receive feedback from many people, but the only feedback that really counts comes from the person in charge. To return to our original illustration, the traditional Roman Catholic rectory: The sisters may think the associate is a wonderful preacher, and the other associates may feel he's a swell guy, but in the long run these opinions don't matter much. What really matters is what the pastor thinks.

In the sovereign style feedback and evaluation are often based on very limited observation, since people working in this style are simply given assignments and then sent off to do them. The person in authority, who provides the feedback, generally does not see all that work and may not, in fact, have a lot to go on in evaluating it. As a result, evaluations may not be very accurate or constructive: They may be based only on occasions when the person in authority happens to be present or on an off-the-job contact. The pastor, for instance, might base his evaluation of the associate more on behavior around the rectory than on actual performance in ministry.

Furthermore, such evaluation tends to be rather judgmental, in the biblical sense of the word *judgment*: That evaluation is a moral, or even final, judgment on whether one is good or bad, saved or condemned, sheep or goat. Thus, people may forget that feedback and evaluation are most constructive when oriented to enabling one's growth and development, based on the presumption that one must always be growing and developing and needs evaluation to make that happen.

In such circumstances, people may come to view evaluation rather negatively. Characteristically, for example, those who have worked under sovereign style for a long time cringe (at least inwardly) at the very word *evaluation*. In many dioceses, any plan for the evaluation of pastors provokes the conscious response, "Who has the right to do that?" The unconscious reaction is fear that anyone might try. Depending on their relationship with the person in authority, subordinates may even come to dread evaluation; they may anticipate it much as they do the dentist's drill.

Finally, sovereign style can induce a curious imbalance between the subjectivity of feedback and evaluation and its moral weight. After all, sovereign style feedback and evaluation reflect only one person's perspective. Those being evaluated might regard such subjective views as something they could take or leave. However, this is seldom possible, given the authority vested in the person doing the evaluating as well as the heavy moral tone which may accompany the process. Although people evaluated in such settings may regard the feedback they receive as insubstantial, they find a take it or leave it response difficult. It can be very hard, for example, simply to dismiss the pastor's opinion.

If parallel style is the main ingredient, feedback and evaluation present quite different difficulties. For one thing, they are usually hidden. Recall that in parallel style people are separated in their work; they go their own ways and do not interact very much. How well one is doing is really no one else's business. Others may make judgments about one's work, or vice versa, but such judgments are generally not shared.

Certainly parallel style does not build in feedback or evaluation, since they would require more interaction than the style allows. Hidden judgments may surface, however, in cases of crisis. As was true of parallel style regarding support and supervision, so also regarding feedback or evaluation: others may rush in if one's piece of the pie begins to collapse. At such times others may not only give support; they may also follow with an evaluation of what went wrong, make judgments about why the crisis arose, and suggest changes one should make to avoid further crisis. Evaluation is thus reduced to the function of crisis management.

Under these circumstances evaluation tends to become personality assessment. When paralleling, people do not see one another's work very much, but they do see one another around the table, the rectory, the faculty lounge. Thus they can evaluate these interactions much more easily than the work itself. If something goes wrong, people must base evaluative judgments on what they know. Perhaps all they have to go on is what they know of the other person from off-the-job contacts. If so, there is a tendency to infer things about one's work performance that are not based on actual observation. What tends to be assessed, then, is not one's performance as a professional, minister, or leader, but what kind of person one is. Judgments about why one is struggling or in crisis may well be irrelevant to one's actual performance. Still, even though the material content may not be relevant, the moral climate (being evaluated by one's peers during a crisis in one's own work) may make it difficult to resist or dismiss even irrelevant feedback. In such cases, feedback and evaluation conceivably do more harm than good.

When semimutual style is the main ingredient in a leadership recipe, feedback and evaluation can become inconsistent and random due to the shifting pattern of interaction. Feedback may come easily when people are working together, on the level of planning. It may, however, prove much more difficult when people are performing particular tasks by themselves.

The specific difficulty in semimutual style is that people who interact only periodically and only on the planning level lack an adequate basis for evaluating one anothers' work. Yet, because each person's work aims to implement goals and objectives originally set by the whole group, others in the group may attempt to make judgments about one's work even though they don't share in the performance of specific tasks.

Furthermore, precisely because it induces others to make judgments based on a relative ignorance of one's actual experience in performing a job, semimutual style is prone to substitute personality assessments for evaluation of job performance—much as is the case with parallel style.

A relative advantage of semimutual over parallel style is the former's tendency for self-correction: Since people do experience constructive feedback and evaluation concerning their behavior on the planning level, this experience may set a standard against which the ignorance-based feedback and evaluation on the tasks level may be exposed as inadequate. Thus people who value the more constructive experience may take steps to make the other, less happy processes measure up. By contrast, parallel style provides no opportunity to create such a discrepancy between two different experiences of feedback and evaluation. Put simply, the tension produced by the shifting pattern of semimutual style may prove, in many settings, to be a creative tension.

People employing mutual style as their main leadership ingredient must regard feedback and evaluation—like support and supervision—not as a luxury or an option, but as part of their standard equipment. Both must be built in if mutual style is to work well.

Indeed, feedback and evaluation may consume a fair portion of the time leaders devote to their work. One of the practical drawbacks of mutual style for many leadership groups is that, however attractive the style may appear in theory, they simply do not have the kind of time for group maintenance (in the form of feedback and evaluation) that the style requires.

Building in feedback as a standard procedure means that the growth and development of each group member becomes the responsibility of all other members: It is part of their work, and may even be written into their job descriptions. In other words, in addition to performing one's own tasks, one assumes responsibility for the on-the-job growth and development of all of one's colleagues. If one is working forty hours per week, for example, a certain amount of time must be set aside for feedback and evaluation (as well as support and supervision). This leaves only so much remaining time for planning and performing one's tasks.

Especially if one is overworked, serving people who need help and depend on one's service—conditions typically present in pastoral ministry—it may seem too much to expect that one also devote time and energy to the needs of one's peers and colleagues. But this is the price one must pay. Without it, group members will lose the bonds that enable them to work together so continually and closely. In practice, this price involves a trade off: The time for one's peers must come out of one's availability to clients, or one will lack the energy to perform well. Too often, people deny this trade off, trying to be completely available to both peers and clients. The result is overextension and burnout. The coin does, of course, have another side: In return for making the trade off, one gets the reciprocal benefit of *receiving* feedback and evaluation (and support and supervision) from colleagues, which otherwise would not be available. Presumably this contributes to one's effectiveness, and even to one's survival in ministry.

A further point: To provide such benefits, feedback and evaluation must focus on performance rather than personality. Since mutual style employs a great deal of joint performance, there is ample data on which colleagues can base such performance assessments. Thus, personality assessments may be set aside in favor of concerns about how one does one's job, where one's strengths and weaknesses lie, and how one may build on strengths while working on weaknesses. This focus is the key to close, ongoing professional bonds among people who practice effective teamwork even though they share neither the intimacy of friendship, nor the commitment of (religious) community, nor the ties of family.

Thus, the intent behind such feedback and evaluation is not just to promote better performance, or even
individual growth and development, but also to create
the kind of relational climate that makes mutual style
tolerable and even enjoyable. Mutual style often
involves interactions laden with vulnerability. Contacts
may become so close, with such tightly connected mov-
ing parts, that the friction could be painful and dangerous without high levels of trust for lubrication.
Feedback and evaluation, properly performed, serve to
promote such trust. Feedback and evaluation of a certain quality are indispensable, then, not as pleasant and
useful options that benefit individuals but as integral
components required by the very nature of mutual
style.

In choosing a main ingredient in one's leadership
style, one must be prepared to consider the issue of
feedback and evaluation. If one chooses mutual style,
successfully implementing that choice *must* include providing for sufficient and effective feedback and evaluation. If one wants other styles, then feedback and
evaluation become options that *may* be added to the
recipe only by overcoming the difficulties posed by the
main ingredient one has chosen. There is no right
answer, no easy option. The minister must choose
deliberately and intentionally what he or she really
wants, knowing what will be required and ready to do it.
The result of such deliberate, intentional, and knowing
choices is a style of leadership that fits one's needs, suits
one's setting, and reflects one's own priorities for pastoral leadership.

Chapter 14

Training

The impact of one's main ingredient on training touches three important areas of pastoral leadership. First, those designing and selecting training programs (whether seminary curricula, formation programs in religious communites, deacon programs, or training for lay people) need to determine how the proposed training actually prepares people for the performance of pastoral leadership. Is the training of sufficiently broad scope to cover all the needed areas of preparation? Is the training of adequate quality? Does the preparation it provides really fit the requirements of the job to be done?

Second, those seeking work in (or hiring someone into) a specific pastoral setting ought to know what type of training would best qualify a candidate, given the unique leadership recipe and main ingredient in that setting.

Third, individuals may want to identify areas of retraining for themselves (in continuing education programs, for example) that might enable them, in a way their original training does not, to be more effective in the style which prevails in their setting.

In any of these areas, the link between one's main ingredient and training may be questioned in two different ways. For each style, one may ask, "What training is needed?" Or for a given training program or experience one may ask, "For which style does this training best prepare one?"

With either line of questioning we should keep in mind a fairly broad understanding of the term *training*. It includes not only (1) the acquisition of certain knowledge and attitudes, but also (2) the mastery of certain skills, and especially (3) socialization to a certain new role as pastoral minister and leader. All three dimensions of training are affected by one's choice of a main ingredient.

For sovereign style ministry, the required knowledge and attitudes are largely theological and hierarchical. One is expected to be well acquainted with the tradition of the Church: its teachings, rites, moral standards, and institutional structure. But beyond theoretical knowledge, one should also know in some practical way how the system of the institutional Church works.

The real training challenge here is to overcome the trainees' innocence. Those entering ministry may already know the legitimating theories that present the institutional Church as divinely guided, but they also ought to realize how human the actual practice of the institution can be. Otherwise, the scandal of confronting the human side of the Church in one's ministry may induce a shock that prevents one from adjusting to one's place in the institution. In my experience such shock—induced by the Church's all too human capacity for insensitivity, immaturity, and even unprofessional and inhuman conduct—accounts for the loss of many lay, religious, and clerical vocations in the last generation. Since the Church *is* human, such fallibility will be with us always, so we can prevent these vocation losses in the future only by training that yields ministers tough and knowing enough to face the Church's humanity.

The skills needed for sovereign style are largely skills for specific ministerial performance: preaching, presiding, hearing confessions, counselling, training catechists, etc. Here again, however, the human institution

of the Church must be faced: Complementing a knowledge of the Church's institutional system should be the
skills enabling one to operate effectively within that
system. In many settings dominated by sovereign style,
these skills have been mastered only on the job as one is
socialized into a "good old boy" network. In a period of
increasing resistance to clericalism (often resisted most
strongly by clerics themselves), this method of learning
institutional skills may appear too exclusive to be a pru-
dent training strategy. It may prove better to provide
opportunities for learning such skills in a forum
(whether in school, in service, or on the job) that does
not require that one be male or ordained. Nonetheless,
this strategy remains typical of many sovereign settings.

The role for which trainees prepare in sovereign style
is the role of a competent and reliable subordinate. One
is not trained to be a superior; such status comes only
with experience and seniority. Thus one must learn
above all to behave according to rank and to respond
according to authority. This involves not only adopting
the appropriate etiquette (of respect, deference, etc.) in
dealing with one's superiors but also accepting that
receiving similar treatment from one's subordinates is
one's due.

There may also be a need for socialization to membership in a specific (religious) community, though this
has not generally been true for diocesan clergy or laity.
An ironic facet of some seminary training has been the
tendency to construct the seminary environment as a
religious community by providing a whole disciplined
way of life for students. In the case of students studying
for diocesan priesthood, this meant being socialized to a
community life they would not find in the rectories to
which they would be assigned after ordination. Thus,
far from socializing them for their ministerial role, such
training raised expectations that the actual role could

not meet. Those who resisted such training often found relief in rectory life; those who valued their training often found rectory life a letdown leading to discontent. A better training strategy would match the style of seminary living to the actual life-style of the practicing minister.

To prepare successfully for parallel style, one must acquire a more detailed knowledge of the specific ministry one intends, since the absence of interaction and supervision may make it difficult to learn from others on the job. It also helps to develop attitudes critical of authority and inclined toward self-sufficiency, since these reflect the experience of paralleling. Self-starters stand out as prime candidates for parallel style, and training for parallel style would do well to highlight self-starting as a primary personal quality for one's professional formation.

The skills training for parallel style must go beyond the specific ministerial skills needed in training for sovereign style. It must also include the development of skills in the management, adminstration, and coordination of programs. Once practicing parallel style, one will become one's own manager, and one cannot rely on a boss, or superior, or pastor to manage things while one ministers. In parallel style, everyone is in charge of his or her own ministry, so the minister's training must include a mastery of the skills needed to take charge.

Socializing trainees for the role of minister in a predominantly parallel setting must focus above all on preparing trainees to cope with the personal and professional burdens peculiar to parallel style: isolation and autonomy. Thus the attitude favoring self-starting mentioned above ought to be bolstered by a formation process that promotes such personal and professional qualities as self-reliance, self-confidence, self-esteem, self-discipline, and assertiveness.

In addition to theological instruction, preparation for semimutual ministry ought to lay heavy stress on building the attitude that *planning* is important in pastoral leadership. For semimutual style is somewhat more oriented to renewal than either sovereign or parallel style; it tends to favor change over stasis, to recognize that leadership ought not be limited to routine maintenance on the one hand and crisis management on the other, but should be expanded to include a more creative and imaginative dimension. What one plans in the group work of semimutual style is neither the routine tasks that will be performed anyhow nor the emergencies one cannot foresee; one plans things that can happen if and only if one decides to make them happen.

Of course, sovereign and parallel leadership may also be creative and imaginative, but they need not be. The point is especially apt regarding parallel style: Often those paralleling have rejected sovereign style as too rigid. Yet many feel that *my* way (which is what one gets in parallel style) may be just as rigid and static as *his* way or *her* way (in sovereign style) ever was. Semimutual style, by contrast, makes little long-term sense if people meet to plan only things that don't require or allow for planning, as must be the case in a completely static setting. Thus training for semimutual style needs to prepare people to look ahead, beyond both the everyday and the unexpected.

It follows that such training must also add to the usual curriculum the mastery of two sets of skills not required by sovereign or parallel styles. First, trainees need to learn how to plan: how to do needs assessments; how to set goals; how to write objectives; how to implement, coordinate, and evaluate plans and programs. Second, they must master skills in group process and group dynamics; since it is groups that perform the planning in semimutual style, it becomes a responsibility of leadership to make sure such groups perform well.

Socializing people for the role of semimutual ministry involves, first, formation for teamwork, since teamwork in planning is what sets semimutual apart from parallel. There is, also, the need to build self-confidence and a sense of autonomy as preparation for carrying out the team's plans. However, anyone eager to ride off alone into the pastoral sunset will soon find that such Lone Ranger ministry and semimutual style don't mix well.

Trainees should also be formed—and if possible practiced—in the role of change agent, since change is the underlying goal that makes planning necessary and valuable. A part of this formation may involve preparing trainees to face unpopularity, resistance, even hostility from those who react negatively when leaders represent not authority but a subversion of the status quo. People inclined to nonconformity make especially good candidates for this role.

Finally, the role suits best those able to relate with yet not depend upon other ministers. Such people combine personal confidence with interpersonal skills to the point where they are equally comfortable planning with others and implementing by themselves.

All of these qualities will come more easily to some personalities than to others, but, given high enough motivation and a genuine willingness to grow, they can be learned by a wide variety of people.

Training for mutual style requires, first, building the attitude that values collaboration not merely because it is practical, useful, or pleasant but because it has value *in itself* (for example, as a reflection of one's view of the Church as community or even as a reflection of one's understanding of the Incarnation). Only such a high, personal priority on collaboration will induce leaders to pay the high price that mutual style demands of those who practice it. Merely thinking of collaboration as a nice ideal will not do. Mutual ministers must regard collaboration as urgent, practical, and of great personal importance.

Furthermore, those preparing for mutual style must acquire (in addition to the areas of knowledge mentioned above for the other styles) a fairly sophisticated understanding of personal development, interpersonal dynamics, and especially such specific dynamics as trust, intimacy, and relational justice. Without such understanding, ministers will be hard pressed to understand what is happening to them and their colleagues once they experience the explosive energies—rooted in the tension between community and individuality—that constant togetherness inevitably unleashes.[1]

Mutual ministry trainees also need to master fairly sophisticated interpersonal and group skills in order to make practical responses to the ongoing dynamics once they understand them. Equally important is a mastery of a style of theological reflection that enables trainees both to view and to use their theological education as a collaborative tool that mobilizes their academic knowledge for the service of their ministry. This is crucial inasmuch as theology informs the motivating worldview of most ministers, and in mutual style that worldview ought not to remain privately held but should become a major feature of the collaborative process.

Teamwork is the keynote of mutual style even more than of semimutual style. Precisely for this reason, however, it is critical in preparing people for mutual style that the role of colleague or team member be distinguished from other roles with which it may be confused. Membership on a mutual style team is not, obviously, the same as holding rank in a hierarchical structure. But neither is it the same as being a family member, nor is it the same as belonging to a community, nor even the same as being friends.

Two dangers result from the failure to distinguish these roles. First, people may gravitate to mutual ministry expecting an experience of, substitute for, or extension of family life, community life, or friendship; this simultaneously imposes unrealistic expectations on mutual style and sets up the individual for disappointment. Second, leaders otherwise attracted to mutual style may avoid it because, even though they are effective as colleagues, they think mutual style requires more than they are prepared to give—namely, that they invest in each other as friends, family, or community as a precondition for mutual style's success. Thus, those training for mutual ministry should be formed in a role that does not need—and should not expect—to depend on colleagues becoming friends, family, or community.

The role of colleague does, however, require many of the personal qualities that also make people good at friendship, family, and community: self-confidence, consistency, flexibility, humor, and above all a genuine humility that allows one simultaneously to be gentle and generous with others (in a way arrogant people are not) and also gentle and generous with oneself (in a way overly modest people are not). In short, although strong friendships, family ties, and community experiences are not built in as part of mutual style, they can provide a powerful foundation for the individuals entering it and even offer clues about an individual's readiness for it.

Two points should be noted about training for leadership in general. First, many of the training requirements for the various styles, far from conflicting, actually accumulate as one moves from sovereign through mutual style. That is to say, the agenda for training, rather than shifting from one focus to another, adds focal points and becomes more complex.

All the styles require theological instruction, for example, but each succeeding style adds further requirements: parallel style adds coordination skills; semimutual style adds a stress on planning; mutual style adds a focus on collaboration. Practically, this means that a single training source (a seminary, for example) could prepare people for a variety of options, not by creating wholly different curricula, but simply by developing a curriculum pluralistic and cumulative enough to provide the variety of learning opportunities relevant to each style.

Second, by now it should be clear that any given experience of training for ministry will, depending on the areas of training it includes or excludes, prepare people better for one style than for others. The logical implication is that one's training should match the style of ministry one practices after training. In the real world, however, this implication is often irrelevant: Many people in ministry have not had much choice about the sort of initial training they received, and many people likewise have had little choice about the leadership style prevailing in the settings where they have worked. Often, therefore, any real match between training and style has been largely accidental.

Nonetheless, the idea of fitting one's training to one's style remains important. For one thing, those conducting training programs may want to review, revise, and develop their curricula to provide for a better fit between the training they offer and the settings for which their trainees prepare. Also, those caught in a mismatch between their training and their setting's style may choose either to retrain, to revise the setting, or to change settings. Which choice works best will depend on circumstances, but any of the three may lead to a better match.

Those who seek to add leaders to their particular setting may find that testing the fit between the setting's style and the candidates' training will provide a helpful screening process. Likewise, people interviewing for a new setting may perform the same test for their own benefit.

Finally, settings in which problems arise among colleagues whose personal styles conflict may find it helpful to seek the conflict's roots in the different training experiences of those colleagues. At the least, people may come to understand better why problems arose; at best, they may identify some common retraining option that might make it easier to work together or even to negotiate a common style.

Put simply, the link between one's training and one's style of leadership in ministry will seldom display the ideal, perfect fit. But attention to that link can often lead to a better way even in the real world in which ministers struggle to serve.

Chapter 15

Creating Your Own
Leadership Recipe

In the Appendix you will find an overview that charts the four basic leadership styles, plus a number of worksheets you can use to create a recipe for leadership style that fits your experience, preferences, personality, ministry, and working conditions.

What is the right recipe for you? As has been emphasized throughout, no one but you can answer that question. There are no general rules that determine the superiority of one recipe over another, since the factors that make a given recipe effective in your setting are unique to your situation.

Still, there are some general guidelines to be followed in developing your recipe. To begin, there are three basic factors governing success with any recipe.

First, you should be intentional about the style you choose. Rather than backing into a corner, or falling into a rut, you should make deliberate decisions about the style of leadership you want. You should know why you want that style, what kind of recipe will provide it, and how you can create it. Perhaps you will only partly succeed in creating the style you want, but such partial success is still better than settling on your style by accident.

Second, you should be consistent in implementing the recipe you have chosen. Your reliability as a leader, both to your colleagues and to your clients, depends on your behaving in a way that is to some extent patterned and predictable. Of course, your recipe may involve using widely different styles in different parts of your work, but the process of shifting from one style to another should follow a sensible pattern rather than a random sequence. A DRE, for instance, might employ sovereign style with office workers, semimutual style with catechists, and parallel style with other professional staff—but these choices should be adhered to consistently. The basic rule of thumb is that, once you settle on a style in relation to any program, group, or client in your ministry, you should stick with that style in all similar cases.

Third, you should be flexible in practicing your style. Without sacrificing consistency you should avoid becoming too rigid, especially if your choices are not working well. The long-term stability of your leadership recipe may require some trial and error at first, or during major transitions, or in dealing with exceptional cases. Your recipe may change and grow as time passes, and flexibility will allow you to grow more effective while challenging you to review periodically to sustain an intentional and consistent recipe.

In addition to these basic factors for ensuring a successful recipe, there are two basic steps in creating that recipe:

First, you need to identify the recipe you want by diagnosing the styles suited to your situation and the best way to mix those styles. This process requires careful reflection on the experience, styles, and preferences of three constituencies: yourself, your present colleagues, and your present setting. In a general way, you know in advance that the best recipe for you is the one that comes closest to satisfying these three constituencies simultaneously. You won't be happy with a recipe that isn't "you," but you won't be effective if the style you choose is unacceptable to your colleagues or incompatible with your setting. The worksheets that follow provide tools for considering the needs of all three constituencies. Use these tools to identify what you want, what your colleagues prefer, and what your setting requires. Only then will you be ready for the following, second step.

Second, you need to implement a recipe that suits you, your colleagues, and your setting. This requires a process of negotiation and planning that deals with several issues: What is the actual recipe currently in use? How did it develop? Is there any consensus favoring a different recipe? What are the differences between the current recipe and the consensus recipe? Can we develop a plan for introducing the changes needed to eliminate these differences?

The worksheets will help you to identify the current recipe, and they will also give you the information you need to see what different recipes you and your colleagues might prefer. It will then be up to you to compare notes, share feelings and values, and take responsibility for building a consensus and a plan for change.

This process may take time, and you may want outside help to facilitate your group's work, but ultimately the results will depend on the limits imposed and the options offered by your setting, your colleagues, and yourself. No one else can do it for you. The renewal of your leadership style, like all renewal, must happen first and finally within *you* and other leaders who are ready and willing, for their own good and the good of all the Church, to take the lead.

Appendix

Overview of the Four Basic Types of Leadership Style

	Examples	Ideals	Characteristics	Relationships
SOVEREIGN	• Traditional R.C. Parish (Pastor and Curates)	• Order and Obedience • Clear Accountability • Uniformity	• Authority Indivisible • Real Delegation Not Common	• Authority • Obedience • Dependence • No Peerage • Respect Rather than Trust
PARALLEL	• "Lone Ranger" Teams • Hospital Chaplains • Military Chaplains • Academic Departments	• Smooth and Complete Division of Labor and Accountability • Autonomy • Responsibility • Diversity	• Task-Oriented • Real Delegation Common • Self-Reliance • No Consensus on Goals and Objectives • No Joint Responsibility for Tasks • Little Interaction	• Peerage via Isolation • Independence • Authority Divided Not Shared • No Need for Trust
SEMIMUTUAL	• Pastor and Board • "Divvied-Up Ministry" Teams	• Clear Division of Labor • Some Joint Accountability • Autonomy Still Stressed • Coordinated Diversity	• Consensus on Goals and Objectives • No Joint Responsibility for Tasks • Periodic (Not Ongoing) Interaction	• Strong Sense of Shared Peerage • Interdependence • Authority Shared • High Trust
MUTUAL	• "Shared Ministry" Teams	• Sharing of Authority, Accountability, Labor • Autonomy Not Stressed • Integration • Diversified Unity	• Consensus on Goals and Objectives • Joint Responsibility for Tasks • Ongoing Interaction	• High Stress (Periodic Interaction Without Ongoing Support) • Two Levels of Peerage: Isolated-Shared • Two Levels of Authority: Divided-Shared • Some Trust

Accountability	Support/Supervision	Feedback/Evaluation	Training
• About (1) Obedience to Authority (2) Support for Agenda of Authority • To Immediate Superior	• Controlled by System • Often Not Given • When Given: (1) Informal, Not Built-in; No Forum (2) Mostly Pastor-Centered (3) Depends on Person, Not System	• Confined to Authority Person's Feedback • Based on Limited Observation • Judgmental (Pass-Fail) • Limited to One Person's Perspective	• Knowledge and Attitudes: Theological and Hierarchical • Skills: (1) Specific Skills for Ministry (2) Operating in Institutional Church • Role: (1) Competent and Reliable Subordinate (2) (Optional) Membership in Community
• Virtually Ruled Out • About Almost Anything • To Self Only	• Gives Little Opportunity • Shows Little Recognition of Need • Sporadic • Problematic: Surfaces "Turf" Issues	• Hidden • None Built-in • Given Only in Relation to Crisis • Judgmental • Vulnerable to Personality Assessments	• Knowledge: Specific Ministry (plus Theological and Hierarchical) • Attitude: Critical of Authority; Self-Sufficient • Skills: Management and Administration • Role: Self-Starter
• To Self Only, for Tasks • To Group, for Plans • Self-Accounting Sometimes Reinforced by General Accounting	• Not Consistent • Restricted to Certain Areas and Issues • Implementational Tasks: Done in Isolation	• Inconsistent, Random • Based on Inadequate Data (No Shared Task Performance) • Vulnerable to Personality Assessments	• Knowledge: Theological and Hierarchical; Specific Ministry • Attitude: Values Planning • Skills: (1) Planning (2) Group Process and Group Dynamics • Role: (1) Source of Creative Imagination/ Change Agent (2) Formation for Teamwork
• About Wide Range of Issues • To Oneself First, Then to Colleagues	• Built-in Systematically • Ongoing, Consistent • Both Formal and Informal • Given for Both Planning and Tasks	• Built-in • Growth and Development of Staff Shared by All • Assesses Performance • Creates Supportive Climate	• Knowledge: Personal Development and Relational Dynamics • Attitude: Values Collaboration *As Such* • Skills: (1) Interpersonal and Group Dynamics (2) Theological Reflection • Role: Full-Time Team Member

Worksheet 1:

Identifying the Recipe You Want

Instructions

1. Each member of the leadership group should take some private time to reflect on the questions below. You may want to consult the book as well as your own experience.
2. The group should gather at a convenient time and place to share reflections. Initially, you should avoid discussing, commenting upon, or responding to each other's input. Just listen.
3. Once all have shared, review what you have heard and list areas of consensus.
4. Open up the discussion to other areas. Use this discussion to test the boundaries and limits of the group's consensus about leadership style.

Questions

1. Think of your *experience* in ministry. In each of the settings you have experienced during your career in ministry, what was the main ingredient in the recipe for leadership?
2. Think of *yourself* as you have developed over the years. What is your own personal preference for a main ingredient?
3. Think of *where you work now*. In your current setting, how would you describe the recipe for leadership?

Worksheet 2:

Your Current Recipe

Instructions

1. Each group member should review each ministerial function listed on Diagnostic Chart A. Cross out any that do not apply. Then add any other functions your work involves.
2. For each function, name the style that is dominant: Sovereign, Parallel, Semimutual, or Mutual.
3. On Diagnostic Chart B, rearrange the results so that all functions using the same style are grouped together.
4. Review these groupings and attempt to describe the recipe profiled in the chart (e.g., "our recipe is *mainly* parallel, with some semimutual and a little sovereign and mutual mixed in").
5. As with Worksheet 1, use your results as the basis for sharing, discussion, and consensus building.

Diagnostic Chart A

Function Area   **Prevailing Style**

1. Assessing needs
2. Goal setting
3. Coordinating
4. Policy making
5. Program planning
6. Conducting programs
7. Evaluation of programs
8. Budget development
9. Expenditure monitoring
10. Personnel: hiring and firing
11. Personnel: supervision
12. Personnel: evaluation
13. Assignment of responsibilities and tasks
14. Staff development and maintenance
15. Purchasing: small
16. Purchasing: large
17. Building maintenance
18. Accountability
19. Bookkeeping/check balancing
20. Bill paying
21. Filing
22. Clerical work
23. General office management
24. Publishing (bulletin, publicity)
25. Fundraising
26.
27.
28.
29.
30.

Diagnostic Chart B

Prevailing Style

Sovereign

Semimutual

Parallel

Mutual

Worksheet 3:

Your Consensus Recipe

Instructions

1. Using Diagnostic Chart A from Worksheet 2 as a reference, add your own particular functions to Design Chart A.
2. For each function, name the style you and your colleagues would like to use in the future. (Some may be the same as in your current recipe; others may change. Where you can't achieve consensus, list all the options different people prefer.)
3. On Design Chart B, rearrange the results so that all functions using the same style are grouped together.
4. Use your results to discuss how the group can implement a new recipe. (You may want to use the issue questions regarding implementation [page 128] as a guide for this discussion.)

Design Chart A

Function Area   **Future Style**

1. Assessing needs
2. Goal setting
3. Coordinating
4. Policy making
5. Program planning
6. Conducting programs
7. Evaluation of programs
8. Budget development
9. Expenditure monitoring
10. Personnel: hiring and firing
11. Personnel: supervision
12. Personnel: evaluation
13. Assignment of responsibilities and tasks
14. Staff development
15. Purchasing: small
16. Purchasing: large
17. Building maintenance
18. Accountability
19. Bookkeeping/check balancing
20. Bill paying
21. Filing
22. Clerical work
23. General office management
24. Publishing (bulletin, publicity)
25. Fundraising
26.
27.
28.
29.
30.

Design Chart B

Future Style

Sovereign

Semimutual

Parallel

Mutual

Notes

Chapter 2: Reform Without Renewal

1. Langdon Gilkey, *Catholicism Confronts Modernity: A Protestant View* (New York: Seabury Press, 1974).
2. Krister Stendahl, "Dean's Report to the President of Harvard College" (Cambridge, Mass.: Harvard Divinity School, 1975-76), 4.

Chapter 7: The Sovereign Style

1. "Readings from Father Hecker," #39, *Paulist Prayer Book* (Ramsey, N.J.: Paulist Press, 1981), 31.

Chapter 10: The Mutual Style

1. From *Called and Gifted: The American Catholic Laity —A Response* (Boston: The Paulist Leadership and Renewal Project, 1981), 3.

Chapter 12: Support and Supervision

1. George I. Hunter, *Theological Field Education* (Newton Centre, Mass.: Boston Theological Institute, 1977), 23.

Chapter 14: Training

1. William Kondrath has suggested that the mutual style's need for such concern about relationships must be met by introducing a different, more feminine voice into formation for ministry. See his "Styles of Ministerial Leadership," in *Human Development*, Vol. 6, No. 3, Fall 1985, 30-33.